# Brazil

# Brazil

BY ANN HEINRICHS

*Enchantment of the World*
*Second Series*

## Children's Press

*An Imprint of Scholastic Inc.*

NEW YORK   TORONTO   LONDON   AUCKLAND   SYDNEY
MEXICO CITY   NEW DELHI   HONG KONG
DANBURY, CONNECTICUT

**Frontispiece:** Rio de Janeiro and Copacabana Beach

*Consultant:* Bill Hinchberger, Publisher, BrazilMax.com

*Please note: All statistics are as up-to-date as possible at the time of publication.*

Book production by Herman Adler

Library of Congress Cataloging-in-Publication Data

Heinrichs, Ann.
  Brazil / by Ann Heinrichs.—Rev. ed.
      p. cm.—(Enchantment of the world. Second series)
  Includes bibliographical references and index.
  ISBN-13: 978-0-516-25014-4
  ISBN-10: 0-516-25014-0
  1. Brazil—Juvenile literature. I. Title. II. Series.
  F2508.5.H45 2007
  981—dc22                    2006036024

SCHOLASTIC, CHILDREN'S PRESS, and associated logos are trademarks and/or registered trademarks of Scholastic Inc.
1 2 3 4 5 6 7 8 9 10 R 17 16 15 14 13 12 11 10 09 08

# Brazil

# Contents

**Cover photo:**
Lily pads

**CHAPTER**

Iguaçu Falls

Blue and gold macaws

# The Many Faces of Brazil

8

THIRTEEN-YEAR-OLD GABRIELA GETS UP AT 5 A.M. FLIES are already buzzing around in her family's two-room house. Their little shack made of wood and mud is home to eight people.

After a half-hour bike ride, Gabriela reaches fields full of long-leafed sisal plants. She cuts down the sharp, spiny sisal leaves and feeds them into a machine that strips off their skin. Next, she gathers the sisal fibers and hangs them up to dry. Eventually, they will be used to make ropes and rugs.

After work, Gabriela rides her bike back into town. There, she attends school for three hours before going home in the evening. Gabriela would rather not work. But if she doesn't, her family will not have enough to eat.

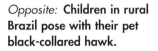

*Opposite:* **Children in rural Brazil pose with their pet black-collared hawk.**

In the countryside, children work on farms with their families. These children are gathering flowers that will be used in crafts.

Seventeen-year-old Alex lives with his parents in a two-story house surrounded by high walls. In the back are a swimming pool and a tennis court. By 7:30 A.M., he arrives at his private school. It is a sprawling complex with a large, tree-lined courtyard.

After his regular classes, Alex spends time in the computer lab, works out with the soccer team, and takes part in school theater productions. University exams are coming up, so he takes extra courses to prepare for them. In his spare time, he likes to practice his guitar, play video games, and go surfing.

Parque Lage in Rio de Janeiro houses an art museum.

Ten-year-old Taki takes careful aim with his bow and arrow. This is his first hunting trip with the men. They move through the forest, listening carefully for barking sounds high in the trees. Taki releases the arrow and hits his mark. As the raccoonlike coati drops to the ground, the men cheer for the young marksman.

A Karajá boy takes aim at a target. About 2,500 Karajá Indians live in central Brazil.

Later, Taki and his friends take off into the jungle. They scramble up trees and swing on liana vines, landing with a splash in the river. In the afternoon, Taki stretches out in a hammock with his pet monkey nestled on his bare chest. He drifts to sleep amid the screeches of birds and the rasp of insects.

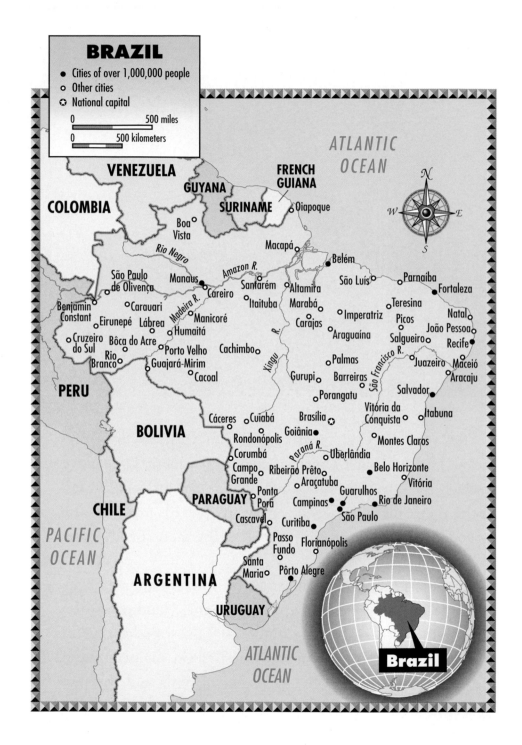

# BRAZIL

- ● Cities of over 1,000,000 people
- ○ Other cities
- ✪ National capital

0            500 miles

0          500 kilometers

ATLANTIC OCEAN

VENEZUELA

GUYANA

FRENCH GUIANA

COLOMBIA

SURINAME

Oiapoque

Boa Vista

Rio Negro

Macapá

Belém

São Paulo de Olivença

Manaus

Amazon R.

Santarém

São Luís

Parnaíba

Fortaleza

Benjamin Constant

Carauari

Madeira R.

Careiro

Itaituba

Altamira

Marabá

Imperatriz

Teresina

Natal

Eirunepé

Lábrea

Manicoré

Carajás

Araguaína

Picos

Salgueiro

João Pessoa

Recife

Cruzeiro do Sul

Humaitá

Bôca do Acre

Porto Velho

Cachimbo

Palmas

São Francisco R.

Juazeiro

Maceió

Rio Branco

Guajará-Mirim

Cacoal

Xingu

Gurupi

Barreiras

Aracaju

PERU

Porangatu

Salvador

Cáceres

Cuiabá

Brasília ✪

Vitória da Conquista

Itabuna

BOLIVIA

Rondonópolis

Goiânia

Montes Claros

Corumbá

Uberlândia

Campo Grande

Ribeirão Prêto

Paraná R.

Araçatuba

Belo Horizonte

Vitória

Ponta Porã

Guarulhos

Rio de Janeiro

PARAGUAY

Campinas

São Paulo

Cascavel

Curitiba

CHILE

Passo Fundo

Florianópolis

PACIFIC OCEAN

Santa Maria

Pôrto Alegre

ARGENTINA

URUGUAY

ATLANTIC OCEAN

Brazil

Gabriela, Alex, and Taki all live in Brazil. In other parts of the country, a child kicks a soccer ball across a dirt lot. Another tumbles through a martial arts routine. One boy swings a machete in a sugarcane field, while another gallops his horse across the plains. One girl picks through a garbage can, while another races her dog along the beach. These children reflect the many lifestyles found in this diverse land.

**Soccer is the most popular sport in Brazil. Children play wherever there is open space.**

Brazil is one of the largest countries on the planet. It covers almost half of the South American continent. Sparkling white-sand beaches line its coast, while dense, tropical forests flourish in the interior. Millions of people visit Brazil every year to enjoy its warm climate and natural beauty. Many come to celebrate Carnival in Rio de Janeiro. One of the world's most famous festivals, Carnival is a whirl of extravagant floats and costumes.

**Dramatic cliffs rise above the sand at Torres. Many people consider it the most beautiful beach in southern Brazil.**

Brazil is home to about 370,000 indigenous people. They speak more than 180 different languages.

Brazil's Amazon rain forest is the largest rain forest on Earth. For thousands of years, it has been home to indigenous (native) people like Taki. In the 1500s, Portuguese settlers made Brazil a colony of Portugal. As more Europeans arrived, they enslaved some Indians and pushed others deeper into the forest. Many settlers became wealthy by growing coffee and sugarcane in Brazil's rich soil. Others prospered by harvesting rubber and trees from the forests or digging for gold in the hills.

Brazilians today are a mixture of European, African, native Indian, and Asian peoples. Each of these groups has woven its own traditions into the fabric of Brazilian life. Whether wealthy like Alex's family or poor like Gabriela's, they share a pride in Brazil's vibrant culture.

# Lush
# Landscapes

A HAWK SOARING HIGH ABOVE BRAZIL WOULD SEE rain forest and desert, green grasslands and murky swamps, sparkling beaches, and even some frosty mountain peaks. Brazil spreads over almost half of South America, so there's plenty of room for these many landscapes. It is the fifth-largest country in the world, after Russia, Canada, China, and the United States.

Brazil is shaped like a diamond, measuring almost exactly the same from north to south and east to west. The eastern half of the country bulges out into the Atlantic Ocean. The

*Opposite:* **Genipabu, in northern Brazil, is famed for its towering sand dunes and sparkling lake.**

**Brazil's 4,655 miles (7,491 km) of coastline include many beautiful beaches.**

Atlantic laps against Brazil's sandy beaches and rocky coasts for more than 4,600 miles (7,400 kilometers). Brazil borders ten other South American countries. The only countries in South America that do not touch Brazil are Ecuador and Chile.

## Brazil's Geographic Features

**Area:** 3,300,171 square miles (8,547,403 sq km)

**Greatest Distance, North to South:** 2,684 miles (4,319 km)

**Greatest Distance, East to West:** 2,689 miles (4,328 km)

**Highest Elevation:** Pico da Neblina, 9,888 feet (3,014 m)

**Lowest Elevation:** Sea level, along the Atlantic coast

**Longest River:** Amazon River, 1,960 miles (3,154 km) within Brazil

**Highest Waterfall:** Iguaçu Falls, 237 feet (72 m)

**Average January Temperatures:**
Manaus, 79°F (26°C)
São Paulo, 70°F (21°C)

**Average July Temperatures:**
Manaus, 80°F (27°C)
São Paulo, 59°F (15°C)

**Average Annual Rainfall:** São Paulo, 55 inches (139 cm)
Western Amazon, more than 160 inches (400 cm)
Northeast interior, 10 inches (26 cm)

The most famous site in Manaus is the opera house, Teatro Amazonas. Most of the materials used to build it were imported from Europe.

## The Amazon Region

The Amazon rain forest covers most of northern Brazil. Through this thick, wet forest flows the mighty Amazon River. In Brazil, this vast rain forest is called Amazônia.

Manaus and Belém are the largest cities in Amazônia. Manaus is the country's major inland port. It lies on a river called the Rio Negro, a few miles from where the Negro joins the Amazon. Manaus is the starting point for many trips into the Amazon region. In the 1890s, men who had grown rich harvesting rubber from trees built Manaus into the "Paris of the Jungle." They even had a grand opera house built there.

Belém sits on the Atlantic coast at the mouth of the Amazon. To the far north lie the Guiana Highlands, which have peaks shrouded in clouds. One of them, Pico da Neblina, is Brazil's highest point.

The planalto stretches across central Brazil. Its flat plains are broken up by cliffs and hills.

## The Northeast

Northeastern Brazil juts out into the Atlantic Ocean. Beaches and farmland line the coast, but much of the interior is an arid plain called the *sertão*. Some cattle are raised here, but the soil is poor for farming. Droughts and floods are common.

About 30 percent of Brazil's people live in the northeast. Its major cities, Salvador and Recife, are on the coast. The northeast was the first center of colonial Brazil. Much of the country's unique flavor—its music, food, and folklore—arose there.

## The Central Plateau

South of the Amazon region is the *planalto*, or central plateau. Brasília, the capital, is a big city stuck in the middle of this empty region. Beyond the city, broad grassy plains are scattered with scrubby trees.

Farther south are rolling hills and rich farmland. Much of this land is carved into huge cattle ranches and plantations. A vast swampland called the Pantanal straddles the Paraguay River of west-central Brazil.

Southern Brazil is prime farmland. Brazil produces more than three million tons of wheat every year.

**The Pantanal**

In western Brazil lies the world's largest wetland, an area where the water is above the ground at least part of the year. The Pantanal covers about 39,000 square miles (101,000 sq km), spilling across the border between Paraguay and Brazil. Hundreds of different animal species thrive in the marshy land. Among them are capybaras, caimans (alligators), giant anteaters, and the jabiru stork, which stands 5 feet (1.5 m) tall.

## The Industrial Heartland

The southeast is the most developed part of Brazil. It has the most fertile farms and pastures, the most productive mines, and almost half the population.

The Brazilian Highlands run from north to south across this region. Their eastern face slopes up steeply from the narrow coastal strip. In earlier years, this mountain barrier blocked people from getting into the interior.

Huge plantations grow coffee and grain in the rich, red soil of southeastern Brazil. The areas around São Paulo and Rio de Janeiro, Brazil's largest cities, are highly industrialized. Belo Horizonte is another center of industry. It lies to the north of Rio de Janeiro, in Minas Gerais state. In colonial times, gold and diamonds were mined in Minas Gerais, which means "General Mines." Now, the region's iron-ore deposits are the basis for Brazil's steel industry.

Rio de Janeiro is sandwiched between the mountains and the sea. The city is an alluring mix of modern skyscrapers and spectacular natural beauty.

## Looking at Brazil's Cities

São Paulo (right) was founded by priests in 1554. Rich coffee barons beautified it with mansions, parks, and museums. Today, São Paulo is Brazil's industrial and financial hub. Avenida Paulista is the major financial street. São Paulo's many ethnic neighborhoods and restaurants reflect its international culture.

Rio de Janeiro, or simply Rio, lies between the sea and a row of sharp mountain peaks. Rio combines excitement, natural beauty, culture, and fun. Both locals and foreigners are drawn to its Carnival festival, forested mountains, and lively beaches such as Copacabana and Ipanema. Sugarloaf Mountain, rising high above Guanabara Bay, can be seen from far out at sea. Another landmark, the huge statue of Christ the Redeemer, looms over Corcovado ("Hunchback") Mountain. Other points of interest are the Botanical Gardens, the Imperial Palace, and the Municipal Theater.

Brazil's African heritage is most visible in Salvador. African influence appears in spicy foods, *Candomblé* religious ceremonies, Afro-Brazilian music, and the martial art of capoeira. Today, Salvador's historic center contains mansions, churches, and public squares from the city's "golden age" as the colony's busiest port.

Belo Horizonte ("Beautiful Horizon") lies in the southeast. It is surrounded by a hilly ridge, which creates the "beautiful horizon" of the city's name. Belo Horizonte is known for its mixture of historic and modern buildings. Among its landmarks are the Mineirão, one of the world's largest sports stadiums, and São Francisco de Assis Church, designed by Brazilian architect Oscar Niemeyer. The city's Savassi district is a center for cultural activities and nightlife.

Fortaleza (left), in northeastern Brazil, grew up around Nossa Senhora da Assunção fort, which was built in the 1600s. The fort remains a major attraction, along with Fortaleza's cathedral, lighthouse, and old docks. The Dragão do Mar Center of Art and Culture is a modern complex with cultural exhibits, a library, and a planetarium. Fortaleza also has many popular beaches. Offshore, fishermen head to work in their traditional fishing boats called *jangadas*.

## Land of the Gaúchos

In southern Brazil, the highlands drop down to broad plains called the pampas. These are grazing lands for thousands of cattle. Gaúchos, Brazil's cowboys, tend the herds on huge ranches there.

Pôrto Alegre is the capital of Rio Grande do Sul, Brazil's southernmost state. It was founded in 1742 by settlers from the Azores, a group of islands in the middle of the Atlantic Ocean. During the 1800s, many immigrants moved to Porto Alegre from Germany and Italy. Rio Grande do Sul's landscape features vineyards, pastures, rocky coastlines, and forested hills. Local industries include making wine and leather goods.

Southern Brazil's major river, the Paraná, forms part of the country's border with Paraguay. Together, the two countries built a powerful hydroelectric power plant, Itaipú Dam, on the Paraná. Only a few miles away is the spectacular Iguaçu Falls, which spills over the border into Argentina.

A gaúcho rounds up cattle in the Pantanal. Some people consider Brazilian beef more healthful than other beef because Brazilian cattle graze on open grasslands.

Countless adventurers have lost their lives exploring the Amazon River. They were foiled by treacherous rapids, fights with native peoples, or starvation. In 1541–1542, the Spaniard Francisco de Orellana became the first explorer to travel from the river's upper reaches to its mouth. Today, ships can easily navigate the Amazon from its mouth all the way to Iquitos, Peru.

From its source in the Andes Mountains, the Amazon courses across the continent for about 4,000 miles (6,400 km).

## Iguaçu Falls

Iguaçu Falls plunges through a gorge across the Brazil-Argentina border. Two hundred seventy-five falls tumble over its horseshoe-shaped rim. They are separated from one another by rocks and islands. *Garganta do Diabo*, or "Devil's Throat," is the most violent drop.

Iguaçu Falls measures about 2 miles (3 km) from side to side. Its waters drop about 237 feet (72 m), sending up walls of foam and spray.

Visitors to Iguaçu Falls can follow trails along the bank for a spectacular view. More adventurous types choose to walk on the *passarelas*. These shaky, wooden catwalks teeter on the edge of the roaring falls. The experience is its own reward—hearing close-up the roar of the thundering water and watching rainbows appear in the spray.

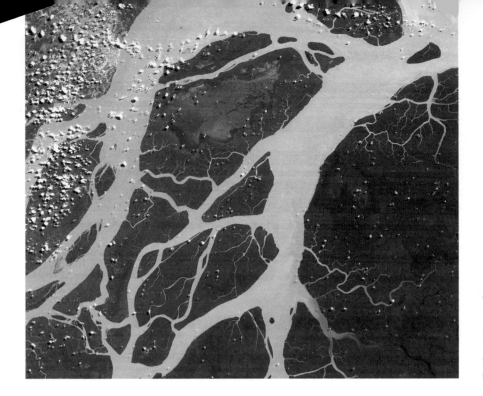

A view of the Amazon River from space. In some places, the Amazon breaks into two main channels, with a maze of smaller streams connecting the two.

It flows through Brazil for 1,960 miles (3,154 km) before reaching the sea. In some places, the Amazon has carved cliffs as deep as 300 feet (90 meters).

The Amazon is the second-longest river in the world; only Africa's Nile River is longer. However, it ranks first among rivers in the amount of water it carries, the number of branches, and the area it drains. One-fifth of the freshwater that enters the world's oceans flows from the mouth of the Amazon. During the rainy season, the river floods, leaving mineral-rich silt behind. This makes for fertile soil. When the Amazon's floodwaters are high, parts of the river are several miles wide. Some early explorers thought the Amazon was a vast inland sea.

More than a thousand rivers and streams flow into the Amazon. The longest of these tributaries is the Madeira River. Another is the Rio Negro, which means "Black River." The

**Sunbathers flock to Ipanema Beach in Rio de Janeiro.**

Rio Negro gets its name from its tea-colored water. The water is dark because of chemicals that seep out of decaying plants in the river.

The São Francisco is the longest river wholly in Brazil. It rises in the southeast, flows east and north, and empties into the Atlantic Ocean. In the south, the Paranaíba and the Rio Grande join to form the Paraná. It flows south into Argentina's Río de la Plata.

## Perfect Climate, Bluest Sky

In 2006, a researcher traveled the world with scientific instruments to measure the "blueness" of the sky in various cities. Rio de Janeiro came in first. It has the bluest sky in the world!

Brazil's climate ranges from warm to hot all year long. It never gets really cold. Visitors and locals alike swear that Brazil has the perfect climate. Most of the country lies south of the equator, the imaginary line that runs around the middle of the globe, so its seasons are the opposite of those in the Northern Hemisphere. In Brazil, June, July, and August are the winter months, while summer comes in December, January, and February.

The hottest areas are those nearest to the equator, which cuts across the northern tip of Brazil. In the northern city of Manaus, the average high temperature in September and October is 92 degrees Fahrenheit (33 degrees Celsius). The northern rain forest is hot and humid, while the northeast and the central plateau are hot and dry. The average temperature in the Amazon basin is 81°F (27°C). The northeast interior is even hotter, often hitting 100°F (38°C). This is the driest region of Brazil. In some places, the annual rainfall is only 10 inches (25 centimeters).

On the southern plateaus the climate is warm and dry. Winters can even be cool. In July, São Paulo's average temperature dips to 59°F (15°C). In the summer month of January, it averages about 70°F (21°C).

Ferns and mosses flourish in Brazil's damp rain forest.

True to its name, the rain forest is wet. Most of the Amazon's rain falls between January and June. The western Amazon region can get more than 160 inches (400 cm) of rain a year. That averages out to almost 0.5 inches (more than 1 cm) every day of the year! Compare this to New York City's annual rainfall of 42 inches (107 cm). The Amazon is almost four times as wet.

In the central and southern plateaus, about 50 inches (125 cm) of rain falls each year, mainly between November and May. Mountains in the south sometimes get frost and snow, but it melts quickly.

# Amazing Wildlife

30

**Brazil's rain forest is famed for its astounding variety of life. Tens of thousands of different species of plants grow there.**

Forests cover half of Brazil, and most are in the hot, humid Amazon region. In the Amazon, the top branches form a canopy, or leafy ceiling, high above the forest floor. Frisky monkeys and brilliantly colored birds dart through the canopy, while millions of creatures scurry around far below. The lush, tropical Amazon jungle is the largest rain forest in the world.

Towering evergreens form the top layer of the forest. Their upper branches spread out and intertwine. Thick vines curl around the trunks and dangle from the limbs. Shorter tree species form the lower layers of greenery. The tangle of leaves is so thick that little light reaches the ground.

There are more tree species in the Amazon rain forest than anywhere else on the planet: as many as three thousand species have been found in 1 square mile (2.6 sq km). Palm, mahogany, rubber, and Brazil-nut trees are some of the best-known varieties.

Rain forest trees are "gardens" for other plants. Their trunks and limbs are covered with mosses, lichens, orchids, and ferns. These plants sink their roots into the rotting leaves and animal droppings that build up on the trees, rather than into soil on the ground.

*Opposite:* **Howler monkeys are the loudest animals in the Western Hemisphere. Their roars can be heard 3 miles (5 km) away.**

### The First Rubber Tappers

Amazon Indians were the first people to process rubber. They cut slashes into rubber trees and collected the white liquid, or latex, that oozed out. This is called rubber tapping. Indians used the latex as an insect repellent and as a waterproof covering for their feathered robes. When heated over a fire, the latex thickened into raw rubber. The people of the Amazon used the rubber to make shoes, bottles, and balls.

## Beasts Above and Below

Jungle animals are most active—and make the most noise—between sunrise and midmorning. As the day gets hotter, they settle down, conserve their energy, and nap. When the sun drops low in the sky, they start up their ruckus again.

**Blue and gold macaws have big, strong beaks that they can use to crack open Brazil nuts.**

Tropical birds are the most colorful creatures in the high canopy. Red, blue, and green parrots, scarlet macaws, and toucans live in the topmost branches. Smaller birds like parakeets, flycatchers, and swifts also flit through the leaves. Hawks and vultures soar overhead, while long-legged herons, ibises, and storks wade along rivers and swamps.

Howler monkeys are the largest monkeys in the Amazon. They get their name from their loud barking and hooting sounds. Capuchins, spider monkeys, and squirrel monkeys are some of the howler's cousins.

Three-toed sloths spend most of their time hanging upside down with their hooked claws. They eat, sleep, and even have their babies in this position. Moths, beetles, and algae live in the sloths' fur. Opossums are "hangers," too. They sleep hanging by their tail all day and forage for fruit and insects at night. Unlike its raccoon relatives, the coati feeds in the daytime.

**Three-toed sloths spend almost their entire lives in trees. They go down to the ground only about once a week.**

Down on the ground are piglike peccaries and tapirs, chunky capybaras, and giant anteaters with big, bushy tails. The capybara is the largest rodent in the world. It looks a bit like a small hippopotamus and weighs more than 100 pounds (45 kilograms).

Any of these animals might make a meal for a jaguar or a black panther. The jaguar is one of the Amazon's many endangered species. One threat to the jaguar is poachers, people who illegally hunt the animals. They make their living by selling the high-priced skins.

**Jaguars are excellent climbers, crawlers, and swimmers. They prey on a wide variety of creatures, from deer to turtles.**

The caiman is a relative of the alligator. Black caimans are becoming rare because they, too, are hunted for their skins. Poachers hunt them at night, scanning the riverbanks with flashlights until they see the creature's shining eyes.

More than two hundred species of snakes live in the Amazon. Boa constrictors and anacondas are the largest. Anacondas grow as long as 40 feet (12 m)—the height of a four-story building! These massive snakes are not poisonous. Instead, they usually squeeze their prey to death and then swallow it whole. Anacondas have been known to swallow an entire cow. It takes days for the snake to digest such a big animal.

**The emerald tree boa swallows it prey whole. After eating a large animal, it can go weeks without eating again.**

## The National Bird

Many Brazilian songs and poems celebrate the *sabiá-laranjeira*, or rufous-bellied thrush. This bird is found throughout the country in forests, parks, and backyards. The sabiá feeds on insects, spiders, coconuts, oranges, and papayas. It spends the winter in Brazil's warm, tropical northern regions and migrates to the more temperate southern zone for the summer. The bird may live as long as twenty-five to thirty years.

Brazil's forests are teeming with insects. Farmers at the forest's edge often find their fence posts shredded by termites, but termites are good for the forest. They add to the nutrients in the soil by eating away at dead trees. The leaf-cutter ant is another forest insect. With their saw-toothed jaws, these ants cut leaves into pieces small enough to carry. Then, in single-file rows, they march the leaf fragments back to their underground colony. There, they chew the leaves into mulch, which they use to feed a fungus that they eat.

Millions of leaf-cutter ants live in a single colony. The ants can remove all the leaves from a tree in a day or two.

## The National Flower

Ipê is the common name for several Brazilian trees. The *ipê-amarelo*, or "yellow ipê," is Brazil's national flower. In September or October, the tree sheds its leaves. Then, its stunning golden blossoms burst into bloom. The tree is used as an ornamental plant in parks and gardens and along roadsides. Its wood is used for posts and fences as well as for cabinetmaking.

## Water Creatures

Piranhas are known for their powerful, razor-toothed jaws. But people in the Amazon region are not afraid of them. They're just very careful. Piranhas attack humans only when their natural food supplies are low. On the other hand, the Amazon's giant, bloodsucking leeches latch on to humans at every opportunity.

The Amazon's pirarucu is the world's largest freshwater fish. Some are 10 feet (3 m) long and weigh 250 pounds (115 kg). The pirarucu is a fruit eater. It springs out of the water to nip fruits from overhanging tree branches.

**Piranhas usually travel in groups of about twenty fish. When they feed, they quickly strip an animal of its flesh, leaving nothing but bones.**

Most dolphins are saltwater creatures that live in the ocean, but the Amazon River region is home to both a gray dolphin and a pink dolphin. The pink dolphin is the subject of many stories. According to an Indian legend, at night it changes into a human and roams the land.

## Medicines from the Forest

One-quarter of the world's medicines come from the rain forest. In fact, many of today's cancer-fighting drugs are made from substances found *only* in tropical rain forests. These medicines are based on extracts from leaves, bark, and insects. Indigenous peoples have used these healing substances for thousands of years. They know which ones to use for snakebites, insect bites, cuts, burns, and countless other problems.

### The Animal Trade

The illegal trade of wild animals is a big business in Brazil. According to Brazil's National Network Against Wild Animal Trafficking, about thirty-eight million wild animals are captured illegally each year. They include parrots, macaws, snakes, monkeys, and turtles.

Some animals go to private collectors and pet shops. Others go to drug companies for scientific research. Only about 10 percent of these captured animals survive the journey from the wild to their final destination. Traffickers sell animal parts, too. Bird feathers, butterfly wings, and turtle shells are made into craft items. Snakes, crocodiles, lizards, and jaguars are valued for their skins.

Several hundred animal-trade gangs operate in Brazil. At one end of the supply chain is a poor Brazilian who needs money. He or she may receive only a few cents for capturing an animal. Payment is sometimes made with alcohol or sacks of rice. The animal passes through a complex network of middlemen before being smuggled out of the country. The final buyer may pay thousands of dollars.

The wild animal trade is the third-largest illegal activity in the world, after the drug trade and the weapons trade. Brazil's environmental police force is working to crack down on animal traffickers, but the problem is so widespread that it's difficult to combat.

Many scientists are studying medicinal plants in the rain forest today. They collect samples of plants used by Indians and then analyze their chemical makeup. The next step is to duplicate these substances in the laboratory so they can be made into medicines that could help people around the world.

One type of araucaria pine is the monkey puzzle tree. It earned this name because its spiky leaves make it difficult to climb.

## Plant Life Beyond the Amazon

Along Brazil's northeastern coast, where less rain falls, the trees are not as tall as rain forest species. Many lose their leaves during the dry season. Brazil's first colonists settled here. Indians showed them how to eat the tangy, pear-shaped fruit of the cashew tree. Hanging at the bottom of each fruit was a bonus—a delicious nut.

Thorny shrubs grow in the *caatinga*, the dry forests of the northeastern backlands. Farther south, in central Brazil, is the *cerrado*, a region with hardy grasses and scrubby trees. More fertile grasslands cover the southeastern plateau.

Flowering bushes and trees add brilliant splashes of color to the southern highlands. *Araucaria* pine trees grow there, too. Sadly, forests are quickly disappearing as they are cut for timber.

**Friends of the Rain Forest**

**Chico Mendes** (1944–1988) was born in Xapuri, in the far west of Brazil. He was a rain forest activist and the leader of the rubber-tappers union. Mendes organized protests against ranchers who were destroying forest-land to turn it into pasture. He was murdered in 1988 by a angry rancher.

**Dorothy Stang** (1931–2005) was an American nun who lived in the Amazon region for more than thirty years. She campaigned for the rights of poor, rural workers and fought to save the rain forest from illegal logging. She was murdered while on her way to a community meeting.

**Marina Silva** (1958– ) is a rubber-tapper's daughter who grew up hunting, fishing, and making rubber. Later, she worked with Chico Mendes in his labor union movement. Silva was elected to Brazil's senate in 1994 and was appointed minister of the environment in 2003. In this position, she has worked hard to protect the rain forest and the indigenous people who live there.

## Vanishing Forests

The Amazon rain forest is shrinking little by little. Loggers, miners, ranchers, and farmers destroy thousands of trees every day.

In the 1970s, mining and logging companies began pushing into the forest. Farmers and ranchers moved in, too. Drought in the northeast was unusually severe, and thousands of poor farmworkers had nowhere to go. Government-sponsored programs made it easy for them to settle in the forest and claim rights to the land. Many people set fire to the forest to clear it for farms and ranches. Day and night, fires raged.

By 1988, the rain forest was disappearing at the rate of 8,300 square miles (21,500 sq km) a year. All over the world, environmentalists were in an uproar. Under pressure from the world community, Brazil began strong conservation programs.

The Amazon region today includes dozens of protected areas such as national parks, biological reserves, and ecological reserves. Strict regulations control activities in the rain forest. Loggers are required to plant new trees wherever they cut. Roads and power plants must be built in ways that preserve the environment.

Illegal cutting and burning continues, however. The forest is too big to police, and everyone knows it. People find ways to get around the laws. Besides, local politicians hate to give up their own region's development in favor of conservation. Government officials hope to strike a balance. They want to use the forest's resources without destroying the forest.

Forests in Brazil are often cut and burned illegally to make room for cattle ranches. In 2006, an area the size of the state of Connecticut was cleared.

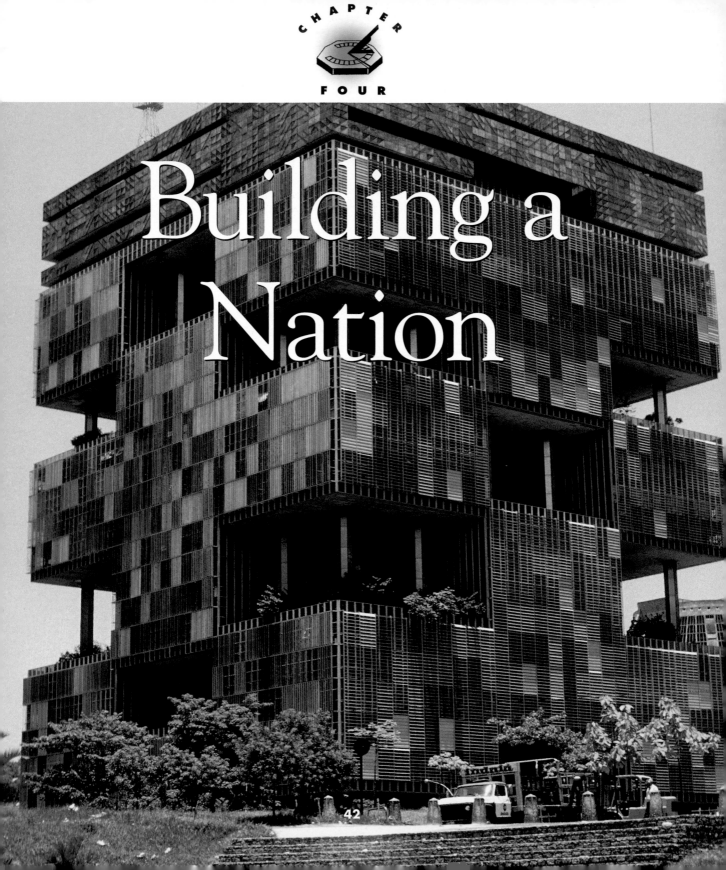

# Building a Nation

MILLIONS OF YEARS AGO, SOUTH AMERICA WAS joined to the continent of Africa. If you compare Brazil's coastline to the west coast of Africa, you can see how they fit together. Eastern Brazil's "bulge" fits right under the "hump" of West Africa. About four hundred million years ago, the two landmasses split and began to drift apart.

Most experts believe people from Asia started migrating into North America around fifteen thousand years ago. They likely crossed a land bridge between what are now Russia and Alaska. In time, people migrated across North America into Central and South America. Brazil's Indians are the descendants of those early migrants.

Around eleven thousand years ago, one group of these Indians lived in a cave at Monte Alegre in the Amazon. Remains found in the cave show that the people ate fruits, fish, shellfish, and large animals. They used tools such as stone spear-points and knives. People later gathered into fishing villages and farming communities.

*Opposite:* **The Petrobras building is one of Rio de Janeiro's most famous modern structures.**

**An ancient rock painting from Monte Alegre**

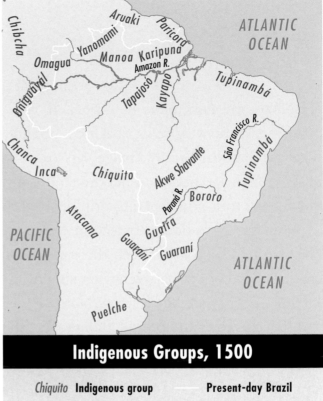

**Indigenous Groups, 1500**

*Chiquito* **Indigenous group** —— **Present-day Brazil**

**The Tupinambá people lived in long huts. Each hut was home to many families.**

Most of Brazil's early indigenous people moved about as they hunted, fished, and gathered wild plants. Others lived in villages of as many as five thousand people. One of their main food sources was a root called manioc, or cassava. Today, manioc is still a common food in Brazil.

### Dividing an Unknown Pie

In the 1400s, explorers from Spain and Portugal were sailing to China and India to trade for spices, silk, pearls, and other goods. On the way, some reached the Americas by accident.

One was Christopher Columbus. He landed on an island a few hundred miles from Brazil. Thinking he had reached the East Indies in Asia, he called the people "Indians."

Soon, Spain and Portugal were in a race to snap up this "New World." Pope Alexander VI, the head of the Roman Catholic Church, stepped in. He took a world map and drew a line through it from north to south. This was called the Line of Demarcation. All lands west of the line would belong to Spain. Those to the east—including eastern Brazil—would be Portugal's. The two countries agreed to this division in the 1494 Treaty of Tordesillas.

Christopher Columbus arrived in the Western Hemisphere in 1492 and began claiming land for Spain. Portuguese explorers would soon follow.

Vicente Yáñez Pinzón
arrived in Brazil in 1500.

Pedro Álvares Cabral
claimed Brazil for
Portugal.

In January 1500, a Spaniard named Vicente Yáñez Pinzón sailed his ship up to the northern coast of what is now Brazil. Though according to the Treaty of Tordesillas, he couldn't claim the land, he is remembered as being the first European to reach Brazil.

Later that same year, Pedro Álvares Cabral set sail from Portugal, headed for India. No one knows why his ships veered toward the southwest, rather than southeast around the tip of Africa. Nevertheless, on April 22, 1500, Cabral spotted the coast of Brazil and landed at what is now Porto Seguro. Cabral had no idea where he was, but he claimed the region for Portugal anyway, naming the land Terra da Vera Cruz ("Land of the True Cross"). He sailed on, leaving two crewmen behind to explore. They were never seen again.

There may have been as many as five million Indians in Brazil when Cabral arrived. The Indians he met along the coast were the Tupinambá. Notes from Cabral's voyage say they wore no clothes but adorned themselves with tattoos and colorful feathers.

The area where Cabral landed became a Portuguese colony, and Portuguese settlers began to move in. As they hacked their way through the forests, they found a tree with bark that made a brilliant red dye. Some said the red tree trunks shimmered like glowing coals in a fire. They called the tree *pau-brasil* ("blazing wood"), or brazilwood. This gave the colony its name, and brazilwood became Brazil's first export.

## Plantations Grow

The colonists found a warm climate and rich soil along the coast of northeastern Brazil. They planted sugarcane on large plantations and shipped sugar back to Europe. Their earliest settlements were Salvador and Recife, and Salvador became the colonial capital.

The Portuguese raided the forests, rounding up Indians to work the fields. But the Indians fought back or ran deeper into the jungle. Many were killed, and entire tribes died of diseases they caught from the settlers. Some Catholic priests tried to protect the Indians from slave raids, but with little success.

The colonists brought in slaves from West Africa as a fresh labor supply. Intermarriage among the Portuguese, Indians, and Africans was common. In time, the mix of races, languages, and customs produced a unique Brazilian culture.

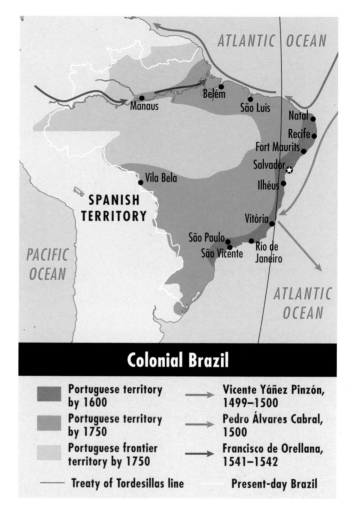

**Colonial Brazil**

- Portuguese territory by 1600
- Portuguese territory by 1750
- Portuguese frontier territory by 1750
- —— Treaty of Tordesillas line
- → Vicente Yáñez Pinzón, 1499–1500
- → Pedro Álvares Cabral, 1500
- → Francisco de Orellana, 1541–1542
- Present-day Brazil

Brazil was the world's major diamond producer in the 1700s. Slaves did all the labor.

### Treasures of the South

In the south, colonists founded the cities of São Vicente and São Paulo. From the coast they pushed inland, clearing paths through the thick forests. Their discoveries—of gold in 1695 and diamonds in 1729—brought a rush of Portuguese fortune hunters who opened mines in the state of Minas Gerais.

Plantations in the south grew a new "boom" crop—coffee. The southern soil favored cotton, too. Cattle ranches sprang up. Rio de Janeiro, perched on a point on the Atlantic, had the best harbor for shipping Brazilian goods. In 1763, Rio de Janeiro became the colony's new capital.

By this time, Portuguese settlers had pushed far beyond the Line of Demarcation and into Spain's territory. In 1777, Portugal and Spain signed the Treaty of San Ildefonso, which set Brazil's borders roughly where they are today.

## The Kingdom of Portugal and Brazil

France invaded Portugal in 1807. For safety, King João VI of Portugal took the royal family and fled to Rio de Janeiro. In 1815, João named his empire the Kingdom of Portugal and Brazil.

João made many changes in Brazil. For the first time, foreigners were allowed to own land. Factories were built and foreign traders came in. Despite these improvements, however, many Brazilians wanted to be free of Portuguese rule. They got their chance in 1821 when João was called back to Portugal. He left his son Pedro in charge.

### Tiradentes: Dentist and Patriot

Tiradentes (1748–1792), or "Tooth Puller," was a dentist who led Brazil's first uprising for independence. Born Joaquim José da Silva Xavier, Tiradentes was inspired by the revolutions in France and the United States. After leading a rebellion in Minas Gerais in 1789, Tiradentes was tried and sentenced to die. His execution day, April 21, is now a national holiday.

## Independence

Pedro was in love with the idea of independence. One day, a Portuguese messenger brought Pedro orders to leave Brazil. As legend has it, Pedro whipped out his sword and cried, "Independence or death!" Brazil declared its independence in 1822, and Pedro was named Emperor Pedro I. In 1831, he gave up the throne and returned to Portugal, leaving behind his five-year-old son. When the boy was fifteen years old, he began his rule as Emperor Pedro II.

**Brazil's First Emperor and Empress**

Pedro I (1798–1834) led Brazilians to independence and became Brazil's first emperor. He was popular for a few years. But then, in a war with Argentina, he lost a Brazilian province that became the nation of Uruguay. Also, citizens resented him for placing Portuguese people in high government positions.

Pedro was forced to give up the throne after nine years as emperor.

Maria Leopoldina (1797–1826) was an archduchess of Austria, who had moved to Brazil to marry Pedro I. She loved Brazil's natural beauty and urged Pedro to make Brazil independent. A neighborhood in Rio de Janeiro is named after her.

Coffee dominated Brazil's economy in the 1800s. It accounted for more than half the country's exports from 1840 to 1890.

During his forty-nine-year reign, Pedro II brought Brazil into the modern world. He started a public school system and built factories to make cotton into cloth. Roads and railroads were built into the interior, and steamships chugged up the Amazon.

Shiploads of European settlers poured in to make their fortune. Many grew coffee in the rich, red soil around São Paulo. Brazil became the foremost coffee producer in the world. Gold mines flourished in the interior, and a new rubber industry sprang up in the Amazon. Brazil was now exporting coffee, rubber, cacao (cocoa), and cattle.

## The Birth of the Republic

Brazil had imported more African slaves than any other country in the world. When Pedro II outlawed slavery in 1888, Brazil became the last nation in the Western Hemisphere to ban slavery. Freeing the slaves, however, enraged Brazil's powerful plantation owners. With the army's help, they forced

Pedro out of the country. On November 15, 1889, Brazil was declared a republic. General Manuel Deodoro da Fonseca, who had led the struggle, became the nation's first president.

The new republic attracted more immigrants than ever before. German, Italian, and Japanese workers poured in to work Brazil's farms and mines in place of the slaves. Some companies even placed ads in foreign newspapers to attract more workers.

Manuel Deodoro da Fonseca was Brazil's first president. He soon declared himself dictator but was then forced from office.

Brazil had a rough time in the early 1900s when Southeast Asia became the world's biggest rubber supplier. The nation's rubber industry crashed as quickly as it had risen. Coffee took its place, soon making up 70 percent of Brazil's exports. But when world coffee prices dropped, the whole country suffered. Amid the chaos, army officers and powerful dictators sometimes took over.

During World War I (1914–1918), industrial countries were busy manufacturing war supplies. This gave Brazil a chance to fill the gap. Factories sped up production, supplying consumer goods to both Brazil and foreign countries.

## The Coffee-and-Milk Republic

Coffee-growing São Paulo and milk-producing Minas Gerais had become Brazil's dominant states. As an unwritten rule, the presidency alternated between candidates from these two regions. This arrangement was known as the Coffee-and-Milk Republic.

In 1930, the outgoing president from São Paulo insisted that another São Paulo candidate succeed him. Breaking the pattern destroyed the republic. Army officers from Minas Gerais banded together with people from other states and took over the government. They made Getúlio Vargas president.

Getúlio Vargas served as president during the Great Depression. He improved health, education, and transportation in Brazil, but he also gave himself the powers of a dictator.

## The Vargas Era

At first, Vargas was committed to expanding the freedoms of the Brazilian people. He allowed workers to join trade unions, so they could demand shorter hours and higher wages as a group. He also expanded voting rights to all adults, including—for the first time—women.

The Great Depression of the 1930s hit Brazil hard, just as it did other countries. Businesses failed, and millions of people were out of work. To Vargas, the situation called for emergency measures. He dissolved Congress, gave himself the powers of a dictator, and canceled many of the freedoms he had helped to create. Vargas used his political power to put people to work and help Brazil out of its economic slump. During this time, new schools, highways, and power plants were built. World War II (1939–1945) gave the nation another boost. Again, Brazil's factories supplied the world with goods that other countries had stopped making. The steel, automobile, and chemical industries boomed. The military eventually removed Vargas, and a new constitution ensured basic freedoms.

## Economic Growth and Military Rule

After the war, foreign companies began to move in and build factories. Juscelino Kubitschek was elected president in 1955. During his term, he had roads and power plants built. He also ordered the construction of the new capital city of Brasília. To make Brazil less dependent on imports, Kubitschek encouraged the steel, automobile, shipbuilding, and machinery industries. In the 1960s and 1970s, the economy boomed.

The good times did not benefit everyone, however. Masses of rural people left their farms and swarmed into the cities to find jobs. With no place to live, they set up shacks on the outskirts of cities. Poverty and unemployment reached emergency levels.

The army had taken over the government again in 1964. Military-backed dictators ruled for the next two decades. During this time, many Brazilians were tortured or imprisoned. Finally, fed up with corrupt officials, civilians took back the government in 1985.

Juscelino Kubitschek became president on the promise that he would build a new capital city. Brasília opened for business just three years after its plans were presented.

## Challenges for the New Democracy

The new democratic government faced staggering problems. To finance its progress, Brazil had borrowed heavily from foreign banks. Now it owed enormous debts. Environmentalists from around the world pressured Brazil to stop clearing its rain forests. Yet Brazil badly needed to develop more land for exports to help pay its debts.

Only in the 1990s did the economy begin to improve. The government cut spending and began transferring government-run industries to private companies. But soon, prices

Fernando Henrique Cordoso served as president for eight years. He is credited with bringing financial stability to Brazil.

were skyrocketing, soaring 5,000 percent in 1993 alone. When Fernando Henrique Cardoso was appointed minister of finance, his main job was to control inflation. Cardoso's 1994 economic program included a new unit of money, the *real*. Within months, Brazil's runaway prices had settled down. Cardoso became president in 1995. As president, he continued to remove industries from state control. He also worked to improve public schools and social conditions.

Brazil still faced many problems, however. Thousands of families in the rural countryside had no farmland, while large private estates owned millions of acres of unused land. The poor staged demonstrations that sometimes ended in bloodshed. Finally, Cardoso agreed to address the problem with new land reform laws.

Luiz Inácio Lula da Silva, who is called Lula, became president in 2003. As a member of the working class himself, he was welcomed as someone who would help the poor. His Zero Hunger program helped millions of Brazilians rise out of poverty. Lula also created many new jobs and raised the minimum wage. Although he moved forward with land reforms, the rural poor complained that he was not moving fast enough. His administration has also been riddled with corruption.

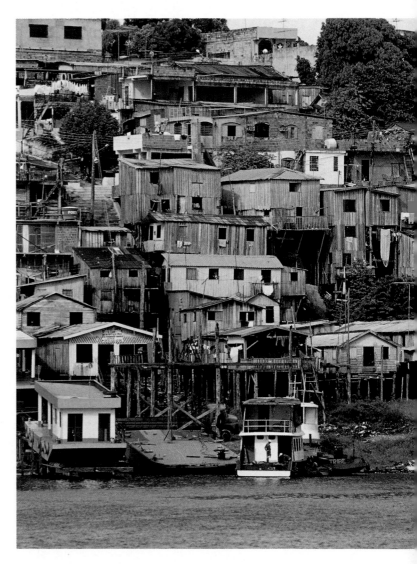

Many Brazilians do not have decent housing. Slums ring all of Brazil's major cities.

### Outlook for the Future

Brazil's economy is expanding. Between the very rich and the very poor is a growing middle class. Still, many problems remain. Battles continue to rage over whether to develop or preserve the rain forest. Cities are plagued with poverty, unemployment, overcrowding, and crime. But Brazilians have a knack for surviving crises. Today, with the steady hand of a stable government, the future looks much brighter than the turbulent past.

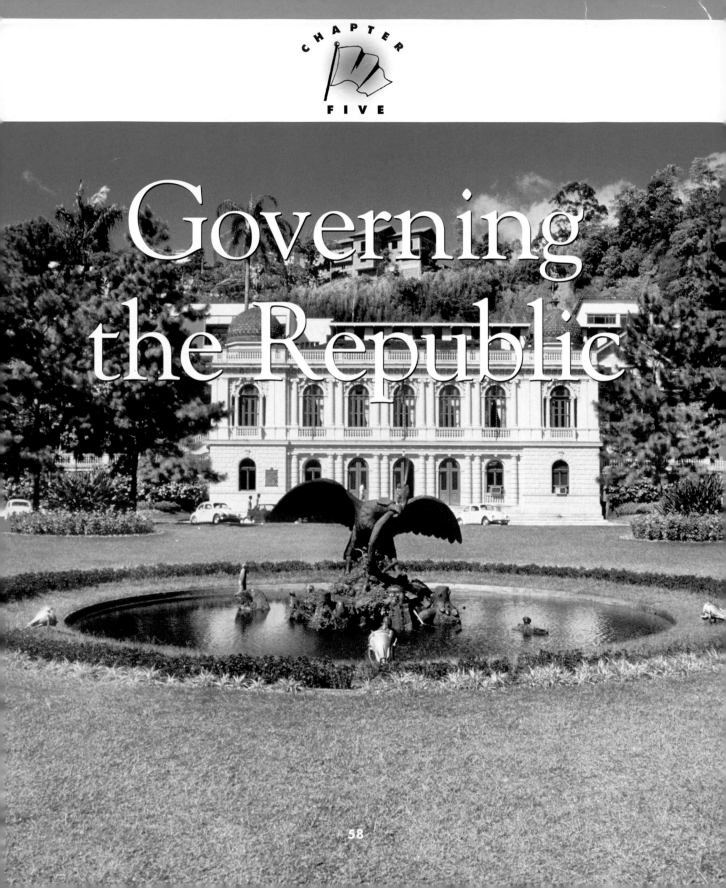

# Governing the Republic

S INCE THE 1500S, BRAZIL HAS BEEN A COLONY, A KING-dom, an empire, and, finally, a republic. Brazil's constitution divides the government into three branches: legislative, executive, and judicial.

*Opposite:* **In the 1800s, Brazil's emperors would retreat to the mountains outside of Rio de Janeiro to escape the heat. Their former summer palace is now a museum.**

## The Legislature

In Brazil, lawmaking power rests in the hands of the National Congress, which is composed of two houses, the Senate and the Chamber of Deputies. Senators must be at least thirty-five years old, while deputies must be at least twenty-one. All members of Congress must be Brazilian-born.

**The National Assembly meets for two sessions every year. If a serious national problem arises, the president or congressional leaders may call a special session.**

The Senate has 81 senators—three from each of the twenty-six states and the federal district. They serve eight-year terms. The 513 members of the Chamber of Deputies are also elected from the states and the federal district. The number of deputies representing a state depends on that state's population. Deputies serve four-year terms.

The Senate and Chamber of Deputies buildings stand side by side in the capital city of Brasília. These ultramodern buildings have been described as looking like two halves of a grapefruit. The Chamber of Deputies faces up and the Senate faces down.

**The National Congress is the centerpiece of Brasília. The Senate and Chamber of Deputies meet in the bowls, while the towers contain offices.**

### Lula: From Poverty to the Presidency

Luiz Inácio Lula da Silva, popularly known as Lula, is Brazil's first working-class president. Previous presidents had come from the upper class or the military. Lula was born in 1945 to poor parents. To help support the family, Lula worked as a shoeshine boy and a street vendor. Later, he became a metalworker. During this time, he became involved in the labor movement. He helped form Brazil's Workers' Party in 1980 and was elected to Congress in 1986.

Lula ran for president in 1989, 1994, and 1998, coming in second each time. Finally, he was elected in 2002. As president, Lula has worked to reduce poverty and keep the economy growing. He was reelected in 2006.

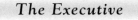

## The Executive

Brazil's president is the chief of state and heads the executive branch of government. Presidential powers are broad. If national security is at stake, the president may impose federal rule on a state.

The president and vice president must be Brazilian-born and at least thirty-five years old. Voters elect both to four-year terms. If no candidate receives more than 50 percent of the vote, the top two candidates run in a second round of elections. The president is limited to two full terms in office.

The president appoints cabinet ministers who give advice in areas such as foreign affairs, labor, and the economy. More advice comes from the Council of the Republic and the National Defense Council. These groups are made up of the vice president, congressional leaders, and cabinet members.

The Supreme Federal Tribunal meets in the Palace of Justice.

## The Judiciary

Brazil's court system makes up the judicial branch of government. The highest court is the Supreme Federal Tribunal, which has eleven judges. The president appoints judges to the Supreme Federal Tribunal and the Senate approves them. The judges are appointed for life.

The Supreme Federal Tribunal hears cases involving high government officials. It judges disputes between state courts and between federal and state courts. Its judges also rule on international lawsuits.

Other federal courts are the Higher Tribunal of

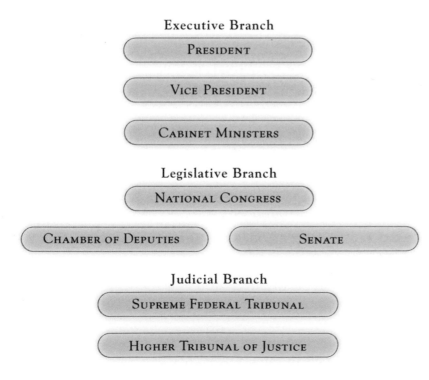

**NATIONAL GOVERNMENT OF BRAZIL**

Executive Branch

PRESIDENT

VICE PRESIDENT

CABINET MINISTERS

Legislative Branch

NATIONAL CONGRESS

CHAMBER OF DEPUTIES        SENATE

Judicial Branch

SUPREME FEDERAL TRIBUNAL

HIGHER TRIBUNAL OF JUSTICE

## Brazil's National Flag

Brazil's flag features a large yellow diamond on a green background. Green stands for Brazil's lush forests and fields. Yellow represents Brazil's rich deposits of gold. In the middle of the diamond is a blue circle representing the night sky. Its twenty-seven white stars stand for Brazil's twenty-six states and the federal district of Brasília. The stars are arranged in the constellations that were visible in the night sky on November 15, 1889—the day Brazil became independent from Portugal. Brazil's motto, *Ordem e Progresso* ("Order and Progress"), is in a white banner across the circle.

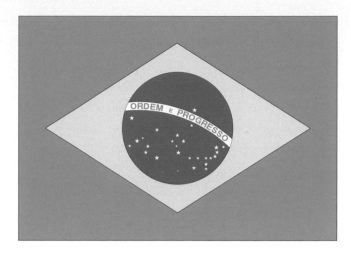

Justice, the Higher Tribunal of Labor, the Higher Tribunal of the Military, and the Higher Tribunal of the Electoral Courts. There are also regional courts in each of these categories. Each state has its own court system.

**The legislature for the state of Rio de Janeiro meets in Tirandentes Palace.**

### State and Local Government

Brazil is divided into twenty-six states and one federal district—the capital city of Brasília. State governments are modeled after the federal government. Voters in each state elect a governor and members of a one-house state legislature. Within each state are small regions called *municípios*, with elected mayors and municipal councils.

## Brazil's National Anthem

The words to "Hino Nacional Brasileiro" ("Brazilian National Anthem") were written by Joaquim Osório Duque Estrada, and the music is by Francisco Manuel da Silva.

### Portuguese lyrics

Ouviram do Ipiranga às margens plácidas
De um povo heróico o brado retumbante,
E o sol da Liberdade, em raios fúlgidos,
Brilhou no céu da Pátria nesse instante.

Se o penhor dessa igualdade
Conseguimos conquistar com braço forte,
Em teu seio, ó Liberdade,
Desafia o nosso peito a própria morte!

Ó Pátria amada, idolatrada,
Salve! Salve!

Brasil um sonho intenso, um raio vívido,
De amor e de esperança à terra desce,
Se em teu formoso céu, risonho e límpido,
A imagem do Cruzeiro resplandece.

Gigante pela própria natureza,
És belo, és forte, impávido colosso,
E o teu futuro espelha essa grandeza.

CHORUS:
Terra adorada! Entre outras mil
És tu, Brasil, Ó Pátria amada!
Dos filhos deste solo és mãe gentil,
Pátria amada, Brasil!

### English lyrics

The peaceful banks of the Ipiranga
Heard the resounding cry of a heroic people,
And the dazzling rays of the sun of Liberty
Bathed our Country in their brilliant light.

If with strong arm we have succeeded
In winning a pledge of equality,
In thy bosom, O Liberty,
Our hearts will defy death itself!

O beloved Homeland, idolized,
All Hail! All Hail!

Brazil, a dream sublime, a vivid ray
Of love and hope to earth descends,
Where in thy clear, pure, beauteous skies
The image of the Southern Cross shines forth.

O country vast by nature,
Fair and strong, a brave colossus,
Thy future mirrors this thy greatness.

CHORUS:
O land adored, among a thousand others,
'Tis thee, Brazil, beloved Homeland!
Thou art the gentle mother of the children of this soil,
Beloved homeland, Brazil!

## Political Parties

Many political parties vie for political power in Brazil. The leading party changes as the people's priorities change.

Some parties favor a strong national government, while others stress states' rights, civil rights, or workers' rights.

The Workers' Party grew in power through the 1990s as the trade union movement gained momentum. In 2002, the Workers' Party won the presidency as well as more seats than any other party in the Chamber of Deputies. Other leading parties include the Social Democratic Party, the Liberal Front Party, the Democratic Movement Party, and the Progressive Party.

At a rally in 1994, Workers' Party supporters carry a picture of future president Luiz Inácio Lula da Silva.

## Voting Rights

In Brazil, young people have a greater voice in their government than those in many other countries. For instance, Brazilians as young as sixteen years old can vote. In the United States and Canada, people cannot vote until they turn eighteen.

By law, all Brazilians between ages eighteen and seventy who can read and write are required to vote. Being unable to read and write does not bar people from voting, but it is optional for them. It is also optional for those under eighteen and over seventy.

## Brasília: Did You Know This?

Brasília, the capital city, stands on a plateau deep in the interior, about 575 miles (925 km) northwest of Rio de Janeiro. Brasília was built far from major population centers in order to attract more people inland and take the crunch off the coastal cities. Brazil's 1891 constitution called for a new federal district to replace Rio de Janeiro. Construction began in 1956. On April 21, 1960, Brasília officially opened for business.

Three designers gave Brasília its sleek, modern look: city planner Lúcio Costa, architect Oscar Niemeyer, and landscape designer Roberto Burle Marx. The city is shaped like an airplane, with government offices forming the central cabin. At the nose is the Square of the Three Powers, where the main executive, legislative, and judicial buildings are located. The airplane's wings are made up of high-rise apartment buildings and businesses.

One of Niemeyer's masterpieces is the National Cathedral, which is shaped like a crown with angels hanging inside. Another is the presidential palace, called the Palace of the Dawn. It is a low, long, glass and marble building that stands on the shore of an artificial lake.

Brasília is a model of modern city design, but it has its drawbacks. As in other Brazilian cities, slums have grown up around the edges. More than 1 million of the city's 2.3 million residents live in these areas. And, with few shade trees to temper the heat, residents avoid the outdoors. Some people who live in the capital miss the vibrant cultural life of the eastern cities and escape to the coast whenever they can.

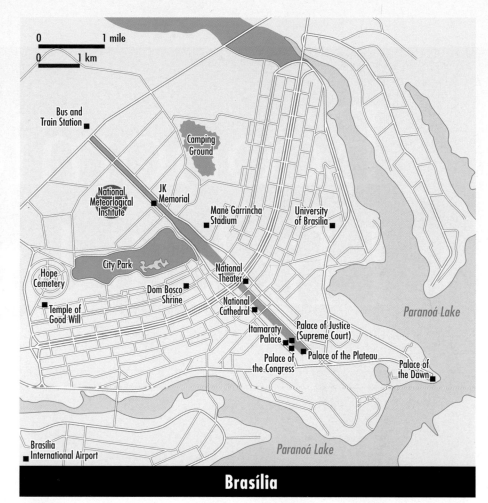

Brasília

# Economic Highlights

Airplanes are made at the Embraer factory in São Paolo.

F ROM THE 1500S UNTIL RECENTLY, A SERIES OF SINGLE products kept the Brazilian economy afloat. At one time or another, it was brazilwood, sugarcane, gold, rubber, and coffee. In the 1940s, the economy began to expand and diversify. New roads and power plants were built, and steel and chemical industries blossomed. Today, Brazil exports everything from airplanes and computers to orange juice and shoes. It has the strongest economy in Central or South America. By the early 2000s, Brazil's economy was the ninth largest in the world.

*Opposite:* **A man holds coffee beans in a sifter. Brazil is the world's top exporter of coffee.**

Favelas have names, just as cities do. Some have uplifting names, like Rio de Janeiro's Cidade de Deus ("City of God") and São Paulo's Paraisópolis ("Paradise City").

## Measures of Wealth

Brazil is a wealthy country in many ways. Its natural resources are lavish, and its economy is large. This does not mean that all Brazilians are rich, however. The wealthiest 10 percent earn almost half of all the income. They include high-ranking government officials and owners of large plantations, ranches, and businesses.

Many Brazilians live in poverty. About one out of twelve people lives on less than one dollar a day. Slums called *favelas* are in every large city. In rural areas, peasants try to eke out a living by farming or fishing. Droughts and floods are constant problems. Many people have no land at all.

In between the rich and the poor is Brazil's middle class. These are businesspeople, government workers, teachers, health-care workers, and other professionals. Service workers such as these make up more than half of Brazil's labor force.

**Brazil has the world's ninth-largest economy. Cities like São Paolo are filled with businesspeople.**

## Manufacturing

Brazil makes cars, trucks, and airplanes for countries all over the world. More than two million motor vehicles roll off its production lines every year. Chemicals, electrical and electronic appliances, machinery, and cement are some of its other factory exports.

Brazil is a world leader in manufacturing. Factory goods make up more than half of Brazil's exports to other countries. Iron and steel products such as cars are the leading manufactures—mainly because the raw materials are local and in good supply. Brazil's iron ore deposits are among the largest in the world.

### Money Facts

Brazil has had seven different currencies since 1986. Since July 1994, Brazil's basic unit of currency has been the *real* (plural *reais*). It is made up of 100 *centavos*. The colorful real bills come in values of 2, 5, 10, 20, 50, and 100 reais. Most bills have images of Brazilian wildlife on the back. For instance, the 5-reais bill shows a great egret, while the 50-reais bill depicts a jaguar. In 2007, 1 real was equal to US$0.48, and US$1.00 was equal to 2.10 reais.

Some farm products also end up in factories. They are turned into orange juice, soy meal, shoes, and clothes. Palm-tree cores are processed and canned as hearts of palm. Much of Brazil's sugarcane is distilled to make fuel.

Most of Brazil's factories are in the south in the states of São Paulo, Rio de Janeiro, Minas Gerais, and Rio Grande do Sul. Volta Redonda's steel plant, near Rio, is the largest in Latin America.

Brazil produces more oranges than any other country in the world. It is also the world's top orange-juice maker.

## What Brazil Grows, Makes, and Mines

**Agriculture (2004)**

| | |
|---|---|
| Sugarcane | 410,983,000 metric tons |
| Soybeans | 49,205,000 metric tons |
| Coffee beans | 2,476,000 metric tons |

**Manufacturing (2004)**

| | |
|---|---|
| Motor vehicles | 2,210,000 units |
| Cement | 34,402,000 metric tons |
| Crude steel | 32,913,000 metric tons |

**Mining (2003)**

| | |
|---|---|
| Iron ore | 234,478,000 metric tons |
| Tin | 11,500,000 metric tons |
| Manganese | 6,500,000 metric tons |

More than 90 percent of Brazil's wheat is grown in the southern state of Paraná.

## Farm and Forest Products

One-third of the world's coffee comes from Brazil, and no other country grows as much sugarcane. But the days of Brazil's one-crop economy are gone forever. Brazil exports more farm products today than any country except the United States.

Soybeans are a valuable export crop. For the most part, they end up as cattle feed. Corn, wheat, and rice are also grown. Cacao and cassava are consumed locally and also exported. One-fourth of the world's beef comes from Brazil's cattle ranches. Chickens, pigs, sheep, and goats are also raised in Brazil.

## A Sweet Solution

In the 1970s, when gasoline prices were rising, Brazil looked for ways to produce cheaper fuel. The country's abundant sugarcane crops provided the solution. Brazil began processing sugarcane to make ethanol, a form of alcohol that can fuel cars. As a result, air pollution from vehicle emissions dropped dramatically. In 2003, Brazil introduced flex-fuel cars—cars than can run on ethanol, gasoline, or a mixture. They soon were outselling gasoline-only cars. Today, no other country in the world produces as much fuel from crops.

Fruits grow well in Brazil's climate. Brazil is the world's top supplier of oranges and papayas. Brazil also grows mangoes, passion fruits, pineapples, lemons, bananas, avocados, and grapes.

Rubber tapping, or extracting latex from rubber trees, provides many people with their only income. Today, many forest products come from plantations instead of from rain forests. They include Brazil nuts, cashews, latex, oils, waxes, gums, and resins.

The Amazon rain forest continues to supply the world demand for fine wood. Mahogany, jacaranda, and teak are some of the major timber woods. Commercial loggers are required to plant new trees where they cut, although some do not. In

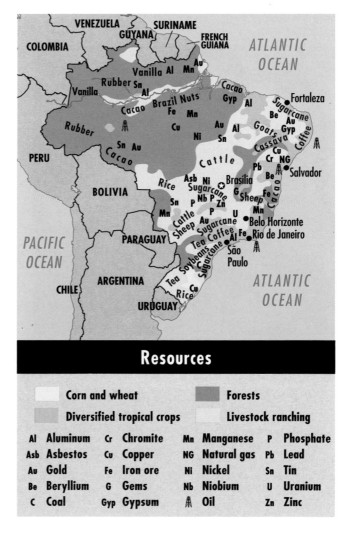

### Resources

| Corn and wheat | Forests |
|---|---|
| Diversified tropical crops | Livestock ranching |

| | | | | | |
|---|---|---|---|---|---|
| Al | Aluminum | Cr | Chromite | Mn | Manganese |
| Asb | Asbestos | Cu | Copper | NG | Natural gas |
| Au | Gold | Fe | Iron ore | Ni | Nickel |
| Be | Beryllium | G | Gems | Nb | Niobium |
| C | Coal | Gyp | Gypsum | Oil | |

| | |
|---|---|
| P | Phosphate |
| Pb | Lead |
| Sn | Tin |
| U | Uranium |
| Zn | Zinc |

the southern forests, araucaria is the most important timber wood. Most is used in construction, and some is made into charcoal for fuel.

## Mining

Brazil is one of the gemstone capitals of the world. Diamonds, emeralds, topazes, amethysts, and aquamarines are all mined there.

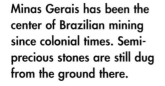

Minas Gerais has been the center of Brazilian mining since colonial times. Semi-precious stones are still dug from the ground there.

With its massive iron deposits, Brazil exports more iron ore than any other country besides Australia. Manganese, tin, and bauxite are also major mining resources. Brazilian mines yield nickel, uranium, copper, lead, and gold. In the 1980s, gold was discovered in the Amazon, starting a gold rush. Deposits of niobium, found in Amazonas state in 1990, are the largest in the world. Niobium is used in making camera lenses, electronic circuits, and many other industrial goods.

## Working Kids

Sixteen is the minimum age for working in Brazil. But in 2001, about 14 percent of children between ten and fifteen years old were in the labor force. Working children in Brazil sweat their childhood away in such places as sugarcane fields, charcoal plants, and tea plantations.

Children in poor families usually start to work at around the age of ten. Their families need their wages to survive. The government has pledged to stop child labor. It has come up with plans to pay families to replace the income they lose when a child stops working and returns to school. Still, many employers—and parents—ignore the guidelines.

## Getting Around

Travel by car is not as widespread in Brazil as it is in the United States and Canada. There is only about one car for every ten people. In the cities, buses and rail lines provide public transportation. Outside the cities, most people travel by bus. In rural areas, people sometimes get around on horseback.

These young boys are making charcoal, a fuel produced by burning wood. An estimated 1.5 million Brazilian children between the ages of five and thirteen work.

Almost 1.1 million miles (1.8 million km) of roads and highways crisscross Brazil, but only about 11 percent of them are paved. Southeastern Brazil has a good road network for its heavy business activity. Modern expressways serve major cities such as Rio and São Paulo.

Roads have been built in the Amazon region, but flooding, potholes, and shaky bridges make them unreliable. Much of the four-lane Trans-Amazon Highway that is supposed to run from Recife to the border with Peru has become overgrown with jungle plants.

**Most of Brazil's rural roads are unpaved.**

The best way to travel into remote Amazon regions is by boat. Large boats can sail the entire length of the Amazon River in Brazil, and oceangoing ships can reach as far as Manaus. Steam-powered boats chug up and down the Amazon River, carrying both cargo and people. Crew members don't bring much food along because they can catch what they need in the river. Rowboats and outboard motorboats are common, too. Indians use canoes made from hollowed-out logs. Even children are experts at steering canoes.

Huge oceangoing container ships carry cargo in and out of Brazil. The busiest port is Santos, which serves São Paulo. Other major ports are Rio de Janeiro and Rio Grande. Within the country, railroads carry freight like iron ore to steel mills and other processing centers.

**Manaus became a major city during the rubber boom of the late 1800s. Today, it is often the starting point for journeys into the Amazon.**

A new airport opened in Recife in 2004.

Brazil has twenty-two international airports. The busiest are in Rio de Janeiro and São Paulo. Airlines such as Varig, TAM, and Gol fly to cities all over Brazil. Countless landing strips have been cleared in the forests, too. They make it

### Alberto Santos-Dumont

Alberto Santos-Dumont (1873–1932) was the first person to make and fly a gasoline-powered aircraft. Santos-Dumont was born and grew up in Brazil. Even as a young man, he was fascinated by the idea of flight. He moved to France in 1891 and in time began designing steerable balloons, or blimps. He piloted his *Airship No. 6* for 7 miles (11 km) in 1901—two years before the Wright brothers flew their first airplane. In 1906, Dumont flew his first gas-powered heavier-than-air machine.

## Telenovelas

*Telenovelas* are the most popular TV shows in Brazil. These dramas are watched by almost three-fourths of Brazilian television viewers. Brazil also exports its telenovelas to other Latin American countries and Europe.

Brazil's telenovelas are often called soap operas, but they're more like TV miniseries. Typically, they last several weeks or months. Telenovelas cover a wide range of subjects on Brazil's history, land, and people. *Terra Nostra* ("Our Land") was about an Italian family that moved to Brazil. *Rei do Gado* ("The Cattle King") was set in cattle territory in the 1800s. *Malhação* ("Working Out"), aimed at teenagers, is Brazil's longest-running telenovela. Debuting in 1995, it was still running in 2007.

easier for scientists to do their work, but they also make life easier for poachers and drug smugglers.

### Spreading the News

More than five hundred daily newspapers are published in Brazil, but no newspaper reaches the whole country. *Fôlha de São Paulo* has the largest circulation, followed by Rio de Janeiro's *O Globo*. Other important dailies are *O Dia* and *O Estado de São Paulo*.

Cell phones are popular in Brazil. About forty-two million land lines are in use, but more than sixty-five million people have cell phones. About twenty-six million Brazilians are Internet users.

*O Globo* is one of Brazil's leading daily newspaper.

# Land of
# Many Peoples

M ORE THAN HALF THE PEOPLE IN SOUTH AMERICA live in Brazil. In fact, only four other countries in the world have a greater population: China, India, the United States, and Indonesia. In 2006, Brazil's population was more than 188 million.

Even with all these people, much of Brazil is thinly populated. That's because most Brazilians live along the coast. About 80 percent of the population live within 200 miles (320 km) of the Atlantic Ocean. By contrast, only about 7 percent of the population live in the vast Amazon region.

About four-fifths of Brazilians live in cities. The largest cities are in the southeast, making for another lopsided statistic: three-fourths of Brazilians live in the southern quarter of the country.

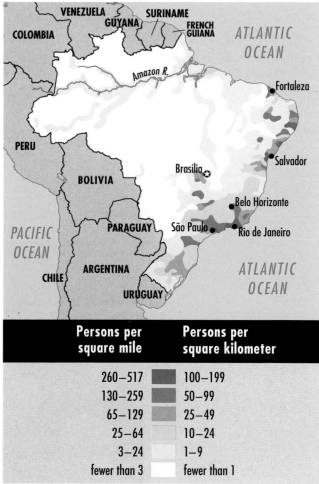

Opposite: **Body paint is common among Brazil's indigenous groups.**

| Persons per square mile | Persons per square kilometer |
|---|---|
| 260–517 | 100–199 |
| 130–259 | 50–99 |
| 65–129 | 25–49 |
| 25–64 | 10–24 |
| 3–24 | 1–9 |
| fewer than 3 | fewer than 1 |

### World-Class Cities

More than ten million people are packed into São Paulo, Brazil's largest city. Counting the suburbs, the metropolitan area is home to more

**Population of
Major Cities
(2004 est.)**

| | |
|---|---|
| São Paulo | 10,838,581 |
| Rio de Janeiro | 6,051,399 |
| Salvador | 2,631,831 |
| Belo Horizonte | 2,350,564 |
| Fortaleza | 2,332,657 |
| Brasília | 2,282,049 |

than eighteen million people. That makes São Paulo the fourth-largest city on the planet. The only cities with higher populations are Tokyo, Japan; Mexico City, Mexico; and New York City.

Rio de Janeiro is Brazil's second-largest city and also one of the largest cities in the world. About six million people live in the city and about eleven million in the metropolitan area.

Why do rural Brazilians leave the wide-open spaces for the crowded cities? They want better jobs, housing, and living

**Sugarloaf Mountain rises across the bay from Rio de Janeiro.**

**Many Brazilians have both black and white ancestors.**

conditions. Cities also offer better health care and nutrition. In general, city residents are healthier and live longer than rural people. Unfortunately, millions of poor city-dwellers end up living in favelas, Brazil's slums. Ramshackle housing, dirty conditions, and rampant crime plague the favelas.

## A Multiracial Society

The mixing of blacks, whites, and Indians in Brazil began almost as soon as the first colonists landed. Today, Brazil is a multiracial society. According to Brazil's 2000 census, about 54 percent of Brazilians are of European ancestry. Most are

**About one-quarter of the people in Brazil are under fifteen years old.**

## Ethnic Brazil (2000 census)

| | |
|---|---|
| European | 53.7% |
| Mixed European and African | 38.5% |
| African | 6.2% |
| Asian | 0.5% |
| Indigenous | 0.4% |
| Not specified | 0.7% |

descended from Portuguese settlers. Others are descendants of immigrants who arrived in the late 1800s and early 1900s. They came from Germany, Italy, Spain, Switzerland, Russia, Poland, and Armenia.

About 39 percent of Brazilians call themselves racially mixed. In reality, most Brazilians of European ancestry also have black or Indian ancestors.

About 6 percent of the population are descendants of African slaves. Their ancestors came from what are now Nigeria, Benin, Angola, and the Congo. Blacks are most numerous in northeastern Brazil. In Bahia state, about 75 percent of the people are black or mixed race.

Many people of Japanese descent also live in Brazil. More Japanese people live in São Paulo than in any other city outside of Japan. Most of the rest of Brazil's Asian population are of Chinese and Korean background. The country is also home to many Lebanese, Syrian, and other Middle Eastern peoples.

Compared to other mixed-race nations, Brazil has few racial problems and little hostility among races. Still, Brazilians with European backgrounds are more likely to get a better education and, therefore, better jobs.

This gate is in a Japanese part of São Paulo. More than one million people of Japanese descent live in the city.

Yanomami women decorate themselves with piercings. Traditionally, they stick three thin sticks through their bottom lip.

## Endangered Cultures

When the Portuguese first arrived in Brazil, about five million people lived there. Brazil's native peoples were organized into about a thousand tribes. Today, only about three hundred thousand Indians live in Brazil—fewer than 1 percent of the population. They belong to about two hundred different tribes. Some of the largest groups are the Guaraní, Yanomami, Tupi, and Ge. Even today, about forty remote tribes have had no contact with outsiders. They live traditional lives of hunting, fishing, gathering, and simple farming.

Most Indians live in the Amazon region in protected areas set aside for them. Indigenous reserves amount to about one-eighth of Brazil's total land area. Indian reserves are meant to protect the Indians. On many reserves, however, the Indians cannot carry on their traditional ways of life. Hunters may be placed on farmland, or farmers may be living on barren soil. As a result, many Indians leave the tribe and move to cities to look for work. In time, the tribe simply disappears.

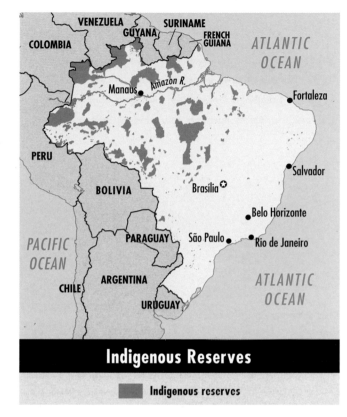

**Indigenous Reserves**

▉ Indigenous reserves

Often, non-Indians illegally take over tribal territories. Illegal logging and gold mining are rampant. Landless peasants take land wherever they can find it. Land-hungry ranchers and plantation owners hire poor people to clear new tracts of land. Some even hire thugs to kill Indians who are in the way. Legal activities can also endanger Indian lands. Farming, gold mining, and ranching pollute streams, killing fish and making the water undrinkable.

Brazil's agency for Indian affairs was established in 1967. It works for the welfare of the nation's indigenous peoples. In 1995, Brazil officially stated that the Indians have rights to lands that they have always occupied and that they need for their traditional way of life. From the Indians' point of view,

### The Yanomami Massacre

When gold was discovered on Yanomami lands in 1987, hordes of gold prospectors invaded the area. In 1993, prospectors murdered seventeen Yanomami Indians in order to mine on their land. Within seven years, between 10 and 15 percent of the entire Yanomami population had been wiped out. The causes included diseases brought by the gold miners, mining pollution, and murder.

however, the government has dragged its feet in this effort and betrayed its promises.

## Education

Brazilian children go to school for four hours a day. Children attend classes in the morning or in the afternoon. Some children spend the rest of the day taking part in sports or clubs.

**Most primary school teachers in Brazil are female.**

Children ages seven to fourteen are required to attend school. In 2003, about 75 percent of high-school-age children were enrolled in school. There are two types of high schools in Brazil. Academic schools prepare students for college, while vocational schools lead directly to jobs.

Brazil offers free education all the way from preschool through college. Brazil has more than 160 colleges and universities. The Federal University of Rio de Janeiro is Brazil's oldest university, and the University of São Paulo is its largest. About half the universities are private Catholic schools. The other half are free public universities. To get into a university, students must take national exams. It's difficult for students who attended public high school to pass those exams, because public schools are not rigorous enough.

The Federal University of Bahia is one of Brazil's top universities. It was founded by the Catholic Church in the 1600s but is now a public university.

Brazil's literacy rate has risen dramatically in recent decades. In 1950, about 50 percent of Brazilian adults could read and write. By 2006, literacy had risen to about 88 percent.

## Language

Almost all Brazilians speak Portuguese, the official language. Brazil is the only country in Latin America where Portuguese is the dominant language. The rest of South America is mainly Spanish-speaking.

Brazilian Portuguese is a little bit different from the language spoken in Portugal—just as American English differs from British English. Several thousand Indian words and many African words found their way into Brazil's Portuguese. The everyday, spoken language is known as *brasileiro falado*. For literary writing, a more formal version is used.

The nation's many indigenous groups speak about 180 different languages. A major language family is Tupi-Guarani. Today, Indian languages, like the Indians themselves, are endangered. Tupinambá, the indigenous language that first influenced Portuguese, is now extinct. Many other languages have died out, and some have only a few living speakers today.

### Common Portuguese Words and Phrases

| | |
|---|---|
| *Sim* | Yes |
| *Não* | No |
| *Por favor* | Please |
| *Olá* | Hello |
| *Adeus* or *tchau* | Good-bye |
| *Como vai?* | How are you? |
| *Eu não entendo.* | I do not understand. |
| *O que é isto?* | What is this? |
| *Onde é . . . ?* | Where is . . . ? |
| *Quanto custa?* | How much does it cost? |

## Big-City Problems

Brazil has nearly four thousand favelas. These slums are home to millions of Brazilians. In São Paulo alone, almost two million people live in favelas, and more people pour in from the countryside every day. Many have no job skills. For housing, they set up cardboard or metal shacks. In some favelas, the government has built public housing. But most of the slums have no electricity, running water, or sewers.

The biggest favela populations are in São Paulo and Rio de Janeiro. But almost all large Brazilian cities have them. Rio's

Rocinha is the largest slum in Rio de Janeiro. A quarter of a million people live there.

favela dwellers face an added danger because they live on hillsides. Landslides during rainy periods can be deadly.

Many government, community, and religious organizations work in the favelas. Some offer education, sports, job-training, and health programs. Others work to improve housing. In 2005, the government began a project to provide water, sewer systems, and home improvement to the favelas. The favela problem is massive, though, and nationwide improvement will take decades.

Street crime is another big-city problem. Gangs of young people from the slums terrorize and rob people on the street. Pickpockets are common, too. Rio has expanded its police department to combat the growing crime problem. The city has also started a special tourist police force. Officers patrol the beaches and other tourist spots in T-shirts that say "I Am Looking Out for You!"

## Street Children

In Brazil, young people wih a difficult home life often end up spending a lot of time on the streets. They are called street children. Most have homes, but some sleep in alleys and doorways, begging or stealing to stay alive.

Many Brazilian police officers treat the street children like criminals. Merchants complain to the police about children begging outside their stores. They are afraid the beggars drive customers away. Police have been known to beat and even kill street children.

Street kids are sometimes called *abandonados*—abandoned

children—but not all are abandoned. It's true that some parents can't feed their children, so they turn them out to fend for themselves. In many cases, the children have been abused at home. They actually feel safer on the streets.

Life on the streets has horrors of its own, though. Some children find work as street vendors or get factory or restaurant jobs, but many are recruited to sell drugs or forced into prostitution. This can be deadly. For Brazilian children ages ten to fourteen, a major cause of death is homicide.

The governments in large cities like Rio de Janeiro and São Paulo are trying to address this problem. International organizations and religious groups have also become involved. Some operate shelters and group homes for homeless kids, while others offer counseling and other services.

**Life is dangerous for Brazil's street children. They are often threatened by the police, and one another.**

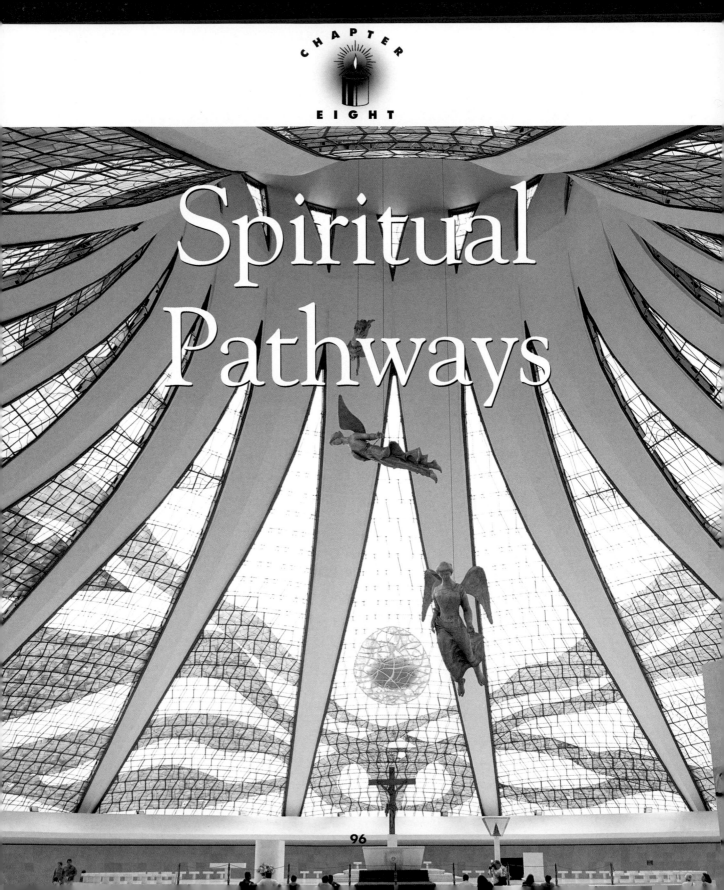

# Spiritual Pathways

Visitors to Brazil see religious symbols and practices of every kind—solemn processions with towering statues, candles glowing on the beach, flowers tossed into the ocean, a mysterious ornament dangling from an old woman's neck. Clearly, Brazilians find many ways to express their spirituality. Religious practices are yet another reflection of Brazil's cultural mix. Many people take part in the ceremonies of more than one religion.

Brazil has no official religion, but almost three-fourths of Brazilians say they are Roman Catholic. Portuguese priests brought the Catholic faith to Brazil in the 1500s. Today, more Catholics live in Brazil than in any other country in the world.

*Opposite:* **The National Cathedral in Brasília was designed to look like a crown.**

**Flowers are brought out to sea during the feast of Iemanjá.**

## Religions of Brazil (2000)

| | |
|---|---|
| Roman Catholic | 73.6% |
| Evangelical Protestant | 15.4% |
| Spiritist | 1.3% |
| Jehovah's Witness | 0.6% |
| Umbanda and Candomblé | 0.3% |
| Buddhist | 0.1% |
| No religion | 7.4% |
| Other and unknown | 1.3% |

Brazil is also home to other Christians, including Anglicans, Lutherans, Methodists, Baptists, and Presbyterians. Evangelical Protestant groups have been growing quickly in recent years. Many of Brazil's Japanese people practice Shinto or Buddhism. Members of the Lebanese and Syrian communities follow Islam or Maronite Catholicism. Brazil is also home to members of the Jehovah's Witness, Jewish, and Baha'i faiths.

## Evangelicals: A Growing Appeal

Brazil has long been a Catholic stronghold, but the number of evangelical Protestants has been rising. In 1991, 84 percent of Brazilians were Catholic, but by 2000, that figure had fallen to about 74 percent. At the same time, evangelical Protestants grew from 9 percent to more than 15 percent of the population.

Evangelical churches are popping up all over Brazil. The largest group, the Assembly of God, has well over eight million members.

Many Brazilians are attracted to evangelical Protestantism because of its dynamic services. The services often include enthusiastic singing and faith healing. The teachings of evangelical churches are very conservative, promoting a strict lifestyle. In a country riddled with corruption, drug problems, and other social ills, this has a strong appeal.

Evangelical missionaries are active in cities and the Amazon region. Among the Indians, they offer important services such as medical care, but the evangelicals are controversial. Critics say they are undermining the Indians' ancient cultures and speeding up the disappearance of already endangered tribes.

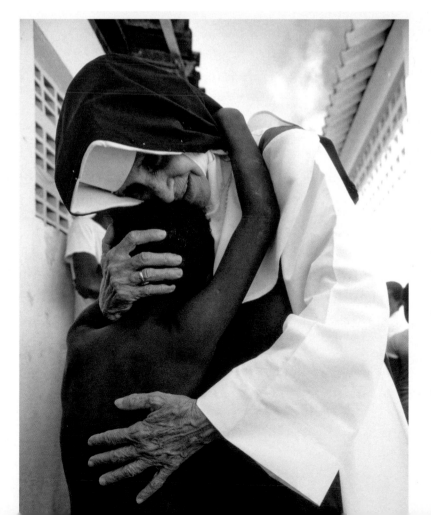

### The Saint of Salvador

Sister Irmã Dulce (1914–1992) was a Catholic nun who spent her life helping the poor in Salvador. Sister Dulce was born Maria Rita Lopes Pontes into a middle-class family. At age thirteen, she resolved to devote her life to the poor. After high school, she became a nun.

Sister Dulce often walked through the streets of Salvador at night, gathering up sick people and beggars to care for. At first, she housed sick people in the convent's chicken coop. Later, she built Santo Antonio Hospital, now the largest hospital in Bahia state. Many Brazilians are hoping the Catholic Church will declare her a saint.

Allen Kardec wrote *The Spirits' Book* in 1857. It laid out the tenets of Spiritism.

## Spiritism

More than two million Brazilians practice Spiritism, or Kardecism. They are followers of Allan Kardec, a nineteenth-century Frenchman. Spiritism centers on a belief in reincarnation, the idea that after a person dies, his or her soul is reborn in a new body. Spiritism also mixes in some traditional Christian beliefs.

Spirtism has broad appeal among educated, middle-class Brazilians. They believe they can communicate with the dead through mediums and heal illnesses through spiritual therapy. Spiritists hold meetings to contact higher beings and find spiritual solutions to problems. They operate hospitals, cultural institutes, research laboratories, and healing centers throughout Brazil.

## Candomblé and Umbanda

Candomblé, a religion that mixes traditional African beliefs with Catholic symbols, is most common in Bahia state. Macumba and Umbanda are variations also found in Brazil.

Candomblé originated among West African people brought to Brazil as slaves. They brought their ancient rituals with them. From the Afro-Brazilian community, Candomblé spread through most levels of Brazilian society. Christian churches have tried to discourage Candomblé, but without much success.

Candomblé ceremonies often take place at night, outdoors, and near a body of water. Participants arrange flowers, candles,

People typically dance all night at Candomblé ceremonies. They believe this helps them connect with the gods.

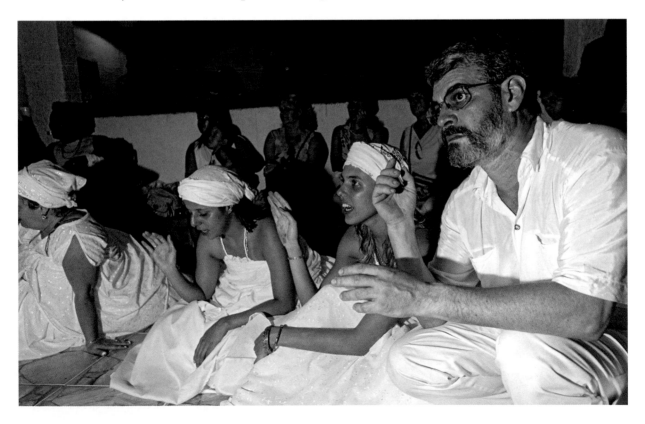

and other objects around the ceremonial site. As drums beat, they chant and dance, calling upon the gods. Some members fall into a trance.

Umbanda originated in Rio de Janeiro in the 1920s. It combines Candomblé, Spiritism, and other African and Brazilian folk beliefs. Like Candomblé, Umbanda is based on the worship of African spirits. These spirits were merged with Catholic religious figures. Oxalá, the god of fertility and harvests, merged with Jesus. Iemanjá, the sea goddess and mother of all other deities, became Mary, the mother of Jesus. Ogum became Saint George, Xangô became Saint Jerome, and so on. Some Indian beliefs were mixed in, too. Umbandists make offerings of candles and food to their spirit protectors, who may be Catholic saints, African gods, or historical heroes. Many use potions to heal illness or bring love.

## Black Saints

Our Lady of the Rosary of the Blacks is a church in the Pelourinho neighborhood of Salvador. The church was built by black slaves working at night. At the time, they were not allowed in churches with white people. Construction on the church began in 1704 and took about a hundred years. Jesus, Mary, and other holy figures in the church are depicted as black.

The feast of Iemanjá celebrates the goddess of the sea. Its roots reach back to the Yoruba people of West Africa.

## Religious Festivals

The *festas juninas*, or June festivals, are especially popular in northeastern Brazil. These holidays celebrate the feasts of Saint Anthony (June 13), Saint John (June 24), and Saint Peter (June 29). Festivities usually start the day before. In some regions, people make the whole month of June a festival time. Saint Anthony is honored with religious devotions, but the other feasts are occasions for fireworks, bonfires, street fairs, dances, and church bazaars.

In Rio de Janeiro, New Year's Eve is also the Umbanda feast of Iemanjá. The candlelight ritual begins at midnight. Thousands of people go down to the beach, toss flowers into the waves, and make good wishes for the New Year. Singing and drumming carry the celebration on through the night. In Bahia, Iemanjá's feast day is February 2. Revelers celebrate that day with a waterfront Candomblé ceremony.

A Yanomami shaman is decorated with sacred symbols. The jar around his neck holds a powder that he takes to bring on visions.

## Indian Spirituality

The Indians' religious beliefs date back thousands of years. For some tribes, the essence of spirituality is honoring their dead. Others practice elaborate rituals to appeal to many spirits and gods.

Most tribes have a story about the beginning of the world that includes a creator or a pair of creators. In a Yanomami story, Omam is the father of the tribe. One day while Omam was fishing, he caught a woman. Their children are the Yanomami people. A giant bird gathered the foam at the water's edge and formed it into other peoples.

From the creator comes the tribe's social structure, wisdom, skills, healing herbs, and way of life. Religious practices are directed not to the creator, but to a variety of spirits. These spirits reside in animals, plants, the Sun and the Moon, and the forces of nature.

The shaman is the tribe's religious leader and healer. He or she performs rites to cure illnesses, bring back lost souls, or drive out evil spirits. Often the shaman uses medicinal plants from the forest.

The whole community sometimes takes part in religious dances. Adorned in body paint and elaborate costumes, they dance for hours—or even days. For some, the object is to ensure a successful hunt. For others, the dance renews their sense of who they are. It keeps them sane in a world that may seem to be spiraling out of control.

Indian religions, like Indian languages, are in decline. Indians who have left their tight-knit communities behind can have a particularly hard time maintaining their religion. Some Indians sell clay figures to tourists but have forgotten what the symbols on the figures mean. Others go off to their factory jobs wearing feathered necklaces, a mix of two very different worlds.

## Mythical Beings

Indian spirit beliefs rubbed off on non-Indians where the two cultures came into contact. Some of these beliefs became part of Brazilian folklore.

The *curupira* is a legendary forest dweller whose feet point backward. He protects the forest from trespassers by confusing them with his backward footprints until they lose their way.

The *boto* is real. It is the pink dolphin of the Amazon River. In legend, the boto changes into a man at night and comes ashore.

To the Indians, *cobra-grande* ("big snake") is the giant serpent of the Amazon, which frightens fishermen away. The Portuguese combined this snake with the European myth of the siren. The result is the Brazilian myth of Iara, a beautiful fish-woman who entices fishermen with her haunting song.

The *saci*, or *saci-pererê*, is a mythical fellow of the central plateaus. He is a one-legged boy with a magic red cap who hops around making mischief and scaring people.

# Sports and Arts

**B**RAZILIANS LOVE SPORTS. THEY BELONG TO THOUSANDS of sports clubs around the country. Most of all, Brazilians are wild about soccer, called *futebol* in Brazil. It's the national sport.

Everyone roots for Brazil's national soccer team, but local teams generate excitement, too. Cities, towns, schools, businesses, and neighborhoods all have soccer teams, and each team has its own pack of loyal, screaming fans. Any patch of dirt is likely to turn into a soccer field.

*Opposite:* **A soccer fan shows her enthusiasm by wearing Brazil's national colors.**

**Soccer is popular everywhere in Brazil, from Rio de Janeiro to the indigenous reserves.**

The biggest event in soccer is the World Cup, a tournament in which national teams from around the world compete. As of 2006, Brazil's national soccer team had won the World Cup championship five times. No other country in the world has won so many times.

Brazil is known for its champion soccer players. Every fan knows about Pelé, Brazil's biggest soccer star of the 1960s. Brazilians still call him "the King." In the early 2000s, the leading soccer star was Ronaldo Luis Nazário de Lima—known simply as Ronaldo. Another favorite is Ronaldinho (Ronaldo de Assis Moreira). Many consider him the best soccer player in the world today.

### Pelé: The King

Edson Arantes do Nascimento (1940– ), better known as Pelé, is considered the world's greatest soccer player of all time. He led Brazil to victory in the World Cup championships of 1958, 1962, and 1970. He became the world's highest-paid athlete when he joined the New York Cosmos in 1975. Pelé, who began playing professionally at age fifteen, scored 1,282 goals during his eighteen-year career.

Nelson Piquet captured the Formula One world championship three times in the 1980s. Today, his son, Nelson Angelo Piquet, is an up-and-coming driver.

## More Sports Highlights

Volleyball, basketball, and auto racing are popular in Brazil, too. With thousands of miles of seafront, millions of Brazilians also enjoy water sports. Surfing, windsurfing, swimming, and fishing are among the national favorites. Other popular sports are skateboarding, hang gliding, and martial arts.

Brazilian athletes have won dozens of medals in the Olympic Games. They have taken home medals in volleyball, beach volleyball, basketball, sailing, running, swimming, judo, and many other sports.

In 1972, at age twenty-five, Brazilian auto racer Emerson Fittipaldi became the youngest-ever Formula One world champion. Fittipaldi took the world championship again in 1974. Two other Brazilians have captured the world title: Nelson Piquet and Ayrton Senna. Brazilians were devastated when thirty-four-year-old Senna was killed in a crash during a race in Italy in 1994.

### The Indigenous Games

Brazil's Indigenous Peoples' Games began in 1996 with just 400 athletes. Ten years later, more than 1,500 athletes were competing. The event, held in a different city each year, features the traditional games of various tribes. One game is *xikunahity*, a type of soccer in which players use only their heads. Another game is *tihimore*, a form of bowling that uses ears of corn as pins. Many other sports, including canoeing, archery, and spear throwing, are also featured.

## Capoeira

*Capoeira* is an Afro-Brazilian martial art that brings together kickboxing, acrobatics, and dance. It was brought to Brazil by West African slaves.

**Capoeirists rarely actually hit each other. Instead, the contest is a demonstration of their moves and skills.**

Capoeira is ritualized and dancelike. Capoeirists use certain basic moves, but every person has an individual style. In a capoeira match, the audience forms a circle around two opponents, who move to rhythmic drumbeats and heroic songs. Capoeira schools are found throughout Brazil, as well as in the United States and Europe.

## Music and Dance

All across Brazil, samba dancers sweat away their spare time. The samba, like much Brazilian music, began with African music and dance rhythms. Many different samba styles developed as Portuguese, Spanish, and pop music mixed with the African beat. Foreigners fell in love with the samba in the 1930s. Dance bands and ballroom dancers in many parts of the world scrambled to learn it.

Northeastern Brazil is the birthplace of *frevo*, a frantic popular dance, and *forró*, a high-powered two-step. *Música sertaneja* is the folksy music of the northeast.

Bossa nova music was born in Rio in the 1950s. Its father was guitarist João Gilberto, who combined jazz with cool, offbeat rhythms. Antônio Carlos Jobim's song "The Girl from Ipanema" launched the bossa nova craze in the United States in 1963.

Gilberto Gil has been a giant of Latin music since the 1960s.

Today, Brazilian pop music is called MPB (for *Música Popular Brasileira*). It is a blend of Western-style pop music and Brazilian rhythms and melodies. Singer-songwriter Gilberto Gil is one of Brazil's most beloved popular musicians. He was appointed Brazil's minister of culture in 2003.

### Teatro Amazonas

Rubber barons built the fabulous Teatro Amazonas in 1896. It stands in Manaus, in the heart of the Amazon rain forest. This ornate opera house features marble from Italy, chandeliers from France, and cast iron from Scotland. Many international opera stars sang there in its early days. Today, the theater has been restored, and some of Europe's finest musicians perform there. It also hosts an annual film festival.

Orchestras around the world play the works of composer Heitor Villa-Lobos. His music is based on Brazilian folk tunes and rhythms. Among his best-known work is a series of pieces known as *Bachianas Brasileiras* ("Brazilian Bach-Pieces").

### Cândido Portinari

Cândido Portinari (1903–1962) painted bold, colorful art in a unique Brazilian style. In his large paintings and murals, he often depicted the lives of Brazil's peasant workers. Portinari painted murals at the Library of Congress in Washington, D.C., and in the United Nations building in New York City.

The finest buildings in Brazil from colonial times are churches. Igreja de São Francisco in Salvador glitters with gold-covered carvings. Minas Gerais has some of the most beautiful colonial churches, built with money from the gold boom. Churches in the town of Ouro Preto are especially ornate. Some are the work of the sculptor Antônio Francisco Lisboa, who carved countless statues out of cedar and soapstone. Lisboa also decorated altars and the outside of churches with elaborate decorations.

In modern times, the best architects in Brazil have worked on all kinds of buildings. Affonso Reidy designed low-income housing outside of Rio, as well as Rio's Museum of Modern Art. In addition to his work on the capital of Brasília, Oscar Niemeyer also designed the Church of St. Francis at Pampulha in Belo Horizonte and helped design the United Nations headquarters in New York City.

Rio de Janeiro's stunning Modern Art Museum is shaped like a spaceship. Its ring of windows offers fantastic views of the water.

## Aleijadinho

Antônio Francisco Lisboa (ca. 1738–1814) is one of Brazil's most famous sculptors and architects. He was nicknamed Aleijadinho, which means "Little Cripple." In midlife, he developed a crippling disease that deformed his body. His chisel had to be strapped to his hand so he could continue working. It was in this condition that he carved what is considered his finest work—*The Twelve Prophets*. This set of sculptures adorns the Sanctuary of Bom Jesus of Matosinhos at Congonhas in Minas Gerais.

## Literature

Brazilian literature in the 1800s was romantic. One of the major trends at this time was called Indianism. Indian themes appeared in poetry, novels, music, and art. José de Alencar's novel *The Guarani* concerns the interaction between a Portuguese family and Indians in early colonial times. It became the basis for an opera by Antônio Carlos Gomes.

In the late 1800s and early 1900s, writers began to portray the harsh realities of the poor. Euclides da Cunha's *Rebellion in the Backlands* is a history of a revolt by a group of peasants. Joaquim Machado de Assis, the son of a freed slave, made fun of Rio's high society in *Epitaph of a Small Winner*. His *Dom Casmurro* became popular all over the world.

Jorge Amado, who died in 2001, was the most famous of Brazil's modern novelists. He wrote about the

Jorge Amado published his first novel at age eighteen.

plight of poor urban people in his native Bahia in *Gabriela, Clove and Cinnamon* and other colorful novels. His novel *Dona Flor and Her Two Husbands* was made into a movie in 1976 and presented as a TV telenovela in 1998. Amado's work has been translated into about fifty languages.

## Ladies of the Silver Screen

**Sônia Braga** (below) was born in 1950 in Maringá, Paraná, and began acting at age fourteen. Children first saw her on Brazil's *Sesame Street* show. Today, she is a TV and movie actress. She became known worldwide for her starring role in *Gabriela*, based on the Jorge Amado novel. Among her American credits are *Moon over Parador*, *Angel Eyes*, and *Che Guevara*.

**Carmen Miranda** (1909–1955), known as "the Brazilian Bombshell," was a popular singer, dancer, and movie actress of the 1940s. She was born Maria do Carmo Miranda da Cunha in Portugal. Her family moved to Brazil when she was a baby. After becoming a star in Brazil, she began touring the United States

in 1939. She dazzled U.S. audiences on stage and in movies, dancing the samba in swirling skirts. Miranda was famous for wearing hats covered with fruit.

**Fernanda Montenegro** (above) is one of Brazil's greatest actresses. She was nominated for an Academy Award as Best Actress in the 1998 movie *Central Station*. Montenegro, who was born in 1929, was the first Latin American actress to receive this honor.

**Xuxa** (pronounced shoo-shah) is Brazil's most popular children's entertainer. Born in 1963 as Maria da Graça Meneghel, she hosted her own children's TV show for many years. Her movies, such as the 2004 *Xuxa and the Mystery of the Lost City*, are typically box-office hits. Xuxa's CDs are also best sellers.

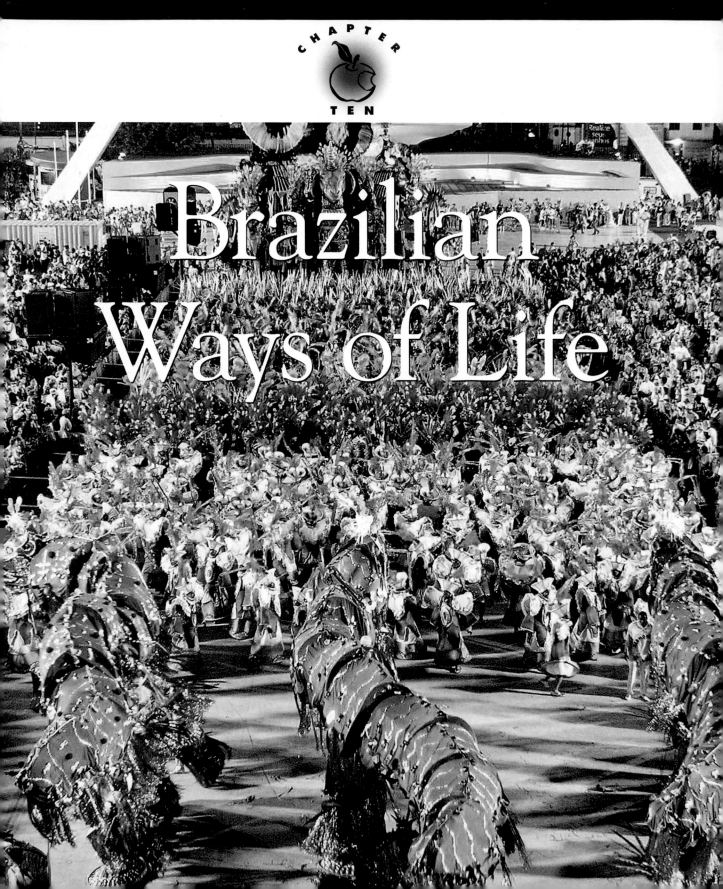

# Brazilian
# Ways of Life

Brazilians TEND TO BE FRIENDLY AND WELCOMING. They often welcome others with open arms—literally. "Hello" and "good-bye" come with handshakes or, among friends, hugs. Women greet each other with kisses on both cheeks. An unmarried woman gets a third kiss for good luck in finding a mate. When Brazilians chat, they often stand close and touch each other.

Visitors from other countries don't always understand these customs. They may feel that Brazilians are invading their space or pledging eternal friendship. For Brazilians, however, these are just casual ways to express their natural warmth.

*Opposite:* **Carnival is an incredible mix of music, dance, and spectacle.**

**Brazilians tend to be warm and sociable.**

There's no snow at Christmastime in Brazil, but many families enjoy traditions such as decorating trees.

Family ties in Brazil are strong. An extended family of three or more generations stays close, often living in the same home. Brazilians trust their family members and count on them for friendship and support. Holidays are times for huge family gatherings, and most leisure time is spent with family members.

Young people begin dating in groups at around age fifteen or sixteen. This gives them a chance to get to know lots of people in a low-pressure setting. In time, they may break off into individual couples. A two- or three-year engagement before marriage is not unusual.

City life in Brazil moves at breakneck speed. The traffic can be terrifying. It's said that normally laid-back Brazilians go wild once they get behind the wheel. High-speed taxi drivers whip around anything in their path. Many drivers step on the gas when they see a yellow traffic light.

Rio de Janeiro has a reputation as being a good place to have fun. In Rio, as in other coastal cities, the beaches are jammed with sunbathers, soccer players, and snack stalls.

Going to the beach is a way of life for many Brazilians. In Rio de Janeiro, it's sometimes hard to find a place to lie down.

Nightlife is serious business. Dinner and dancing start late and can last all night. In São Paulo, life is more geared to business and industry. Culture, entertainment, and faces in the crowds reflect dozens of nationalities.

People from the state of São Paulo are called *Paulistas*, and the people of Rio de Janeiro are called *Cariocas*. Showing the stereotype of the two places, Brazilians like to quip: "Paulistas work, while Cariocas play."

Throughout Brazil, shops usually stay open from 8 A.M. to 6 P.M. on weekdays and 8 A.M. to noon on Saturdays. Some businesses close from noon till 2 P.M. for a long lunch break. Lunch (*almoço*) is served between 11:30 A.M. and 3 P.M. Dinner (*jantar*) is late—7 to 11 P.M. Brazilians keep time on the twenty-four-hour clock. For example, three o'clock in the afternoon is 15:00.

**Shoppers crowd a market in Manaus.**

Feijoada is a hearty mixture of black beans and sausage or other meats. It is often served with cooked greens and orange slices.

## A World of Food Choices

Indigenous, African, and Portuguese food mingle on the dinner tables of Brazil. Meat, rice, and black beans are basic ingredients, along with fresh fruits and vegetables.

*Feijoada* is the national dish. It's a hearty stew of meat, black beans, and rice. Lunch is the time for feijoada, and Saturday is the day to eat it. At home, Brazilians fuss over their preparations and invite guests over for hours of eating. Some restaurants fix huge pots of feijoada and serve it all day long.

West Africans gave Brazilian food its spicy flavors and its big-pot style. Slaves had a "cooking-pot" tradition, tossing leftovers and local produce into a big pot on the fire. They often used coconut milk, palm oil, and peppers.

African influence is strongest in the foods of Bahia. Specialties include *vatapá* (shrimp, fish, dendê palm oil, and coconut milk) and *carurú* (shrimp, okra, and red pepper sauce). In the open-air markets, Bahian women in flowing dresses cook *acarajé* (fried black-eyed pea cakes) in big pots.

*Churrasco* is the regional favorite in the south. It is made of beef chunks grilled on long skewers. Out on the range, gaúchos make churrasco by roasting an entire steer over a fire pit. In the churrasco restaurants of Rio Grande do Sul, the food comes with a stage show of local song and dance.

Most churrasco restaurants are all-you-can-eat. Waiters keep bringing meat to the table until the customers say they've had enough.

## Table Manners

From the Indians came sweet potatoes, hearts of palm, manioc, and chocolate. In the Amazon region, some choice dishes are *pato no tucupi* (duck in a hot, green-herb sauce) and *tacacá* (yellow shrimp-and-garlic soup).

The Portuguese brought food traditions to Brazil, too. Their coffee, syrupy desserts, and dried fruits came from the North Africans who once occupied Portugal and Spain. In Brazil, colonists made the same foods, only with local ingredients. Brazilian desserts include "angel's belly" (egg yolks and sugar), "angel's chin" (syrup-coated tarts), "maiden's drool" (coconut pudding), "kisses of a farmer's daughter" (coconut cakes), and "mother-in-law's eyes" (prunes stuffed with coconut paste).

Immigrants added more food choices in Brazil. Germans brought schnitzel, sausages, and strudel. Japanese brought sushi (raw fish), and Spaniards brought paella (a seafood stew).

Brazilians drink *cafezinho* (strong black coffee), *café com leite* (coffee with milk), or a tea called *maté*. There are tropical fruit juices galore. An Amazon fruit called *guaraná* is made into a popular soft drink.

## A Place to Call Home

Middle-class Brazilians rent apartments in high-rise buildings or own houses in the suburbs. The upper class lives in elegant

condos or palace-like homes. Some have high iron fences and armed guards to protect themselves and their property.

In startling contrast are the favelas on the hillsides in Rio. They look right down on luxury condos and hotels. In some favelas, living conditions are dangerous or unhealthy. Houses in some favelas are built on stilts over streams of sewage. Those on hillsides are in danger of being washed away by landslides. Still, many longtime favela residents take pride in their homes. They keep them neat and paint them bright colors.

Ranch and plantation owners live in rambling houses with wide, covered porches. In the rural northeast, home is a one- or two-room house made of stone or mud bricks with a tile roof. Near rivers and swamps, houses are built on high poles.

Indians build shelters of sapling trunks or cane stalks. Roofs are made of palm branches. "Furniture" is a hammock strung between poles. Some tribes live in villages of thatched-roof huts built in a circle around a central area.

*Malocas*, in the northwest Amazon, are large, round communal houses, some with more than one hundred residents. Each family has its own space, though there are no inside walls. The Indians don't need walls to separate themselves from one another. Mutual respect is all they need to establish their own home space.

## Living on Stilts

Some houses in the Amazon region are built high above the ground on stilts. This protects the homes from high floodwaters during rainy seasons. The houses often have thatched roofs and walls of woven palm leaves. Schools are built on stilts, too. When the water level is high, kids row to school in boats.

## National Holidays

| | |
|---|---|
| New Year's Day | January 1 |
| Carnival | Late February or early March |
| Good Friday | Friday before Easter |
| Tiradentes Day | April 21 |
| Labor Day | May 1 |
| Ascension Day | Forty days after Easter |
| Corpus Christi | May or June |
| Independence Day | September 7 |
| Our Lady of Aparecida | October 12 |
| All Souls' Day | November 2 |
| Day of the Republic | November 15 |
| Christmas | December 25 |

### Carnaval

In all of Brazil, the biggest, wildest festival is Carnival (*Carnaval* in Portuguese). It's a last fling before the somber, pre-Easter season of Lent. Carnival usually takes place in late February or early March, but people begin preparing for it right after Christmas. They're busy designing costumes, building floats, and attending costume balls.

Rio de Janeiro's Carnival is the most spectacular. Tourists come from all over the world to enjoy the costumes, parades, flashy dancers, round-the-clock parties, and nonstop music. All over town, people in sequins, feathers, and wild makeup jam streets and ballrooms. The samba schools' parade is the biggest attraction. Crowds pack the grandstands along the parade route to watch the floats and dancers compete for first prize.

Salvador and Olinda have famous celebrations also. In Salvador, the high point of Carnival is the Electric Trio Parade. Bands on flatbed trucks put on fantastic sound-and-light shows, thrilling delirious crowds. The Puppet Parade opens Carnival in Olinda. Puppet clubs march through the city with papier-mâché puppets 15 feet (5 m) high.

At the stroke of midnight on the Tuesday before Ash Wednesday—the beginning of Lent—the festival abruptly ends. Street sweepers begin their cleanup, and everyone goes home to sleep. Many, no doubt, are dreaming of next year's Carnival.

*Opposite:* **Parades take over the streets of Rio de Janeiro during Carnival. The parades feature massive bands, huge floats, and thousands of dancers in wild costumes.**

# Timeline

## Brazil's History

Early peoples migrate to the Amazon **ca. 9000** B.C.

The Treaty of Tordesillas divides the     A.D. **1494**
Americas between Spain and Portugal.

Portuguese explorer Pedro Álvarez Cabral     **1500**
lands in Brazil and claims it for Portugal.

Rio de Janeiro is founded.     **1565**

Gold is discovered in Minas Gerais.     **1695**

Rio de Janeiro becomes the capital     **1763**
of Brazil.

Spain and Portugal sign the Treaty of     **1777**
San Ildefonso, which sets Brazil's borders
roughly where they are today.

## World History

**2500** B.C.    Egyptians build the pyramids
and the Sphinx in Giza.

**563** B.C.    The Buddha is born in India.

A.D. **313**    The Roman emperor Constantine
legalizes Christianity.

**610**    The Prophet Muhammad begins preaching
a new religion called Islam.

**1054**    The Eastern (Orthodox) and Western
(Roman Catholic) Churches break apart.

**1095**    The Crusades begin.

**1215**    King John seals the Magna Carta.

**1300s**    The Renaissance begins in Italy.

**1347**    The plague sweeps through Europe.

**1453**    Ottoman Turks capture Constantinople,
conquering the Byzantine Empire.

**1492**    Columbus arrives in North America.

**1500s**    Reformers break away from the Catholic
Church, and Protestantism is born.

**1776**    The U.S. Declaration of Independence
is signed.

## Brazil's History

| | |
|---|---|
| Tiradentes leads the first major rebellion against Portugal's rule. | 1789 |
| The Portuguese royal family leaves for Brazil after France invades Portugal. | 1807 |
| Pedro declares the independent Empire of Brazil, with himself as emperor. | 1822 |
| Slavery is abolished in Brazil. | 1888 |
| Brazil becomes a republic. | 1889 |
| A revolt puts Getúlio Vargas in power. | 1930 |
| Brasília becomes the capital. | 1960 |
| A military dictatorship begins. | 1964 |
| Free elections mark the return of democracy in Brazil. | 1985 |
| A new constitution is adopted. | 1988 |
| Brazil wins its fifth World Cup soccer victory. | 2002 |
| Luiz Inácio Lula da Silva (Lula) becomes Brazil's first working-class president. | 2003 |

## World History

| | |
|---|---|
| 1789 | The French Revolution begins. |
| 1865 | The American Civil War ends. |
| 1879 | The first practical light bulb is invented. |
| 1914 | World War I begins. |
| 1917 | The Bolshevik Revolution brings communism to Russia. |
| 1929 | A worldwide economic depression begins. |
| 1939 | World War II begins. |
| 1945 | World War II ends. |
| 1957 | The Vietnam War begins. |
| 1969 | Humans land on the Moon. |
| 1975 | The Vietnam War ends. |
| 1989 | The Berlin Wall is torn down as communism crumbles in Eastern Europe. |
| 1991 | The Soviet Union breaks into separate states. |
| 2001 | Terrorists attack the World Trade Center in New York City and the Pentagon in Washington, D.C. |

# Fast Facts

**Official name:** Federative Republic of Brazil

**Capital:** Brasília

**Official language:** Portuguese

Brasília

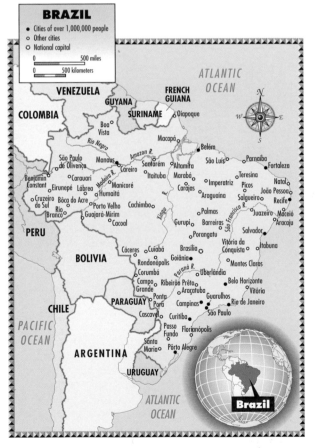

Brazil's flag

Torres

| | |
|---|---|
| **Official religion:** | None |
| **Founding date:** | 1822 |
| **Founder:** | Dom João IV of Portugal |
| **National anthem:** | "Hino Nacional Brasileiro" ("Brazilian National Anthem") |
| **Government:** | Federal republic |
| **Chief of state:** | President |
| **Head of government:** | President |
| **Area:** | 3,300,171 square miles (8,547,403 sq km) |
| **Greatest distances:** | North to south, 2,684 miles (4,319 km) East to west, 2,689 miles (4,328 km) |
| **Coordinates of geographic center:** | 10°00'S, 55°00'W |
| **Bordering countries:** | French Guiana, Suriname, Guyana, Venezuela, Colombia, Peru, Bolivia, Paraguay, Argentina, and Uruguay |
| **Highest elevation:** | Pico da Neblina, 9,888 feet (3,014 m) |
| **Lowest elevation:** | Sea level, along the coast |

**Average temperatures:**

| | January | July |
|---|---|---|
| Manaus | 79°F (26°C) | 80°F (27°C) |
| São Paulo | 70°F (21°C) | 59°F (15°C) |

**Average annual rainfall:**

São Paulo, 55 inches (139 cm)
Western Amazon, more than 160 inches (400 cm)
Northeast interior, 10 inches (26 cm)

Rain forest

| | |
|---|---|
| **National population (2006 est.):** | 188,000,000 |

| **Population of largest cities (2004 est):** | | |
|---|---|---|
| | São Paulo | 10,838,581 |
| | Rio de Janeiro | 6,051,399 |
| | Salvador | 2,631,831 |
| | Belo Horizonte | 2,350,564 |
| | Fortaleza | 2,332,657 |
| | Brasília | 2,282,049 |

**Famous landmarks:** ▶ *Amazon rain forest*, in the western interior

▶ *Itaipú Dam*, on the Paraná River

▶ *Sugarloaf Mountain*, Rio de Janeiro

▶ *Christ the Redeemer statue*, Rio de Janeiro

▶ *National Cathedral*, Brasília

**Industry:** Brazil has the ninth-largest economy in the world. More than half of Brazilian workers are employed in service industries, such as government, education, health care, and trade. Manufacturing also plays a major role in the economy. Cars, iron and steel, cement, and foods are the major products. Agriculture, forestry, and fishing make up 8 percent of Brazil's economic production. Coffee, soybeans, oranges, and sugarcane are the most important crops.

**Currency:** Brazil's basic unit of currency is the real. In 2007, 1 real equaled US$0.48, and US$1.00 equaled 2.10 reais.

**Weights and measures:** Metric system

**Adult literacy rate:** 88%

Currency

Rural children

Jorge Amado

**Common words and phrases:**

| | |
|---|---|
| *Sim* | Yes |
| *Não* | No |
| *Por favor* | Please |
| *Olá* | Hello |
| *Adeus* or *tchau* | Good-bye |
| *Como vai?* | How are you? |
| *Eu não entendo.* | I do not understand. |
| *O que é isto?* | What is this? |
| *Onde é . . . ?* | Where is . . . ? |
| *Quanto custa?* | How much does it cost? |

**Famous Brazilians:**

Jorge Amado      (1912–2001)
*Novelist*

João Gilberto      (1931– )
*Musician and composer*

João VI      (1769–1826)
*King of Portugal and Brazil*

Antônio Carlos Jobim      (1927–1994)
*Musician and composer*

Joaquim Maria Machado de Assis   (1839–1908)
*Novelist and poet*

Carmen Miranda      (1909–1955)
*Singer and actress*

Pedro I      (1798–1834)
*First emperor of Brazil*

Pelé (Edson Arantes do Nascimento)   (1940– )
*Soccer star*

Alberto Santos-Dumont      (1873–1932)
*Aviation pioneer*

Getúlio Vargas      (1882–1954)
*President*

# To Find Out More

## Books

▶ Barter, James. *Rivers of the World: The Amazon*. San Diego: Lucent Books, 2002.

▶ Costain, Meredith, and Paul Collins. *Welcome to Brazil*. Philadelphia: Chelsea House, 2001.

▶ Hollander, Malika. *Brazil: The Culture*. New York: Crabtree, 2003.

▶ Morrison, Marion. *Brazil*. North Mankato, MN: Smart Apple Media, 2003.

▶ Scoones, Simon. *Focus on Brazil*. Milwaukee: World Almanac Library, 2007.

▶ Sharp, Anne Wallace. *Indigenous Peoples of the World: The Amazon*. San Diego: Lucent Books, 2004.

▶ Streissguth, Thomas. *Brazil in Pictures*. Minneapolis: Lerner Publications, 2003.

▶ Tahan, Raya. *The Yanomami of Brazil*. Minneapolis: Lerner Publications, 2002.

▶ Watson, Galadriel. *The Amazon Rainforest: The Largest Rainforest in the World*. New York: Weigl, 2005.

## Video

▶ *Experience Northeast Brazil*. VHS. 47 minutes. Lonely Planet, 1997.

▶ *Families of Brazil*. DVD. 30 minutes. Master Communications, 2006.

## Web Sites

▶ **Brazilian Culture**
http://www.brazilsf.org/brazil_culture_eng.htm
*To learn about Brazilian art, music, drama, and dance.*

▶ **BrazilMax**
http://www.brazilmax.com
*For information about travel, culture, nature, and history.*

▶ **Maria-Brazil**
http://www.maria-brazil.org
*To find out about Brazil's music, folklore, foods, and interesting places.*

▶ **Time for Kids: Brazil**
http://www.timeforkids.com /TFK/specials/goplaces/ 0,12405,104221,00.html
*To meet rain forest animals, see famous landmarks, and learn about the lives of some real Brazilian kids.*

## Organizations and Embassies

▶ **Brazilian Embassy**
3006 Massachusetts Avenue NW
Washington, DC 20008
202-238-2700
http://www.brasilemb.org

▶ **Brazilian Tourism Office**
2141 Wisconsin Ave NW, Suite E-2
Washington, DC 20007
800-727-2945
http://www.braziltourism.org

▶ **Embassy of Brazil – Ottawa**
450 Wilbrod Street
Ottawa, Ontario, Canada
K1N 6M8
613-237-1090
http://www.brasembottawa.org/

# Index

Page numbers in *italics*
indicate illustrations.

# Meet the Author

Ann Heinrichs fell in love with faraway places as a child while reading Doctor Doolittle books and *Peter Freuchen's Book of the Seven Seas*. As an adult, her travels have taken her through most of the United States and much of Europe, as well as to Africa, the Middle East, and East Asia.

"Research trips are fun," she says, "but much of my hardcore research happens at the library. When I begin a book, I head straight for the reference department. Some of my favorite resources are United Nations publications, *Europa World Yearbook*, and periodicals databases."

Ann prefers writing nonfiction rather than fiction. "I guess I'm a frustrated journalist," she says. "I'm driven to track down facts and present them in an engaging way. For me, facts are more exciting than fiction, and I want my readers to experience a subject as passionately as I do. Also, I feel it's vital for American kids to understand unfamiliar cultures, so I like to report on what kids in another country are doing—to tell about their interests, values, and daily lives, as well as their economic role in the family."

Ann, grew up roaming the woods of Arkansas. Now, she lives in Chicago, Illinois. After pursuing successful careers as an editor and an advertising copywriter, she is now the author of more than two hundred books for children and young adults on American, European, Asian, and African history and culture. She holds bachelor's and master's degrees in piano performance. More recently, her performing arts are t'ai chi empty-hand and sword forms. She is an award-winning martial artist and has participated in regional and national tournaments.

# Photo Credits